Katharine of Aragon: Henry VIII's First Wife

A Tudor Times Insight

By Tudor Times

Published by Tudor Times Ltd

Tudor Times Insights

Tudor Times Insights are books collating articles from our website www.tudortimes.co.uk which is a repository for a wide variety of information about the Tudor and Stewart period 1485 – 1625. There you can find material on People, Places, Daily Life, Military & Warfare, Politics & Economics and Religion. The site has a Book Review section, with author interviews and a book club. It also features comprehensive family trees, and a 'What's On' event list with information about forthcoming activities relevant to the Tudors and Stewarts.

Titles in the Series

Profiles

Katherine Parr: Henry VIII's Sixth Queen

James IV: King of Scots

Lady Margaret Pole: Countess of Salisbury

Thomas Wolsey: Henry VIII's Cardinal

Marie of Guise: Regent of Scotland

Thomas Cromwell: Henry VIII's Chief Minister

Lady Penelope Devereux: Sir Philip Sidney's Muse

James V: Scotland's Renaissance King

Lady Katherine Grey: Tudor Prisoner

Sir William Cecil: Elizabeth I's Chief Minister

Lady Margaret Douglas: Countess of Lennox

Sir James Melville: Scottish Ambassador

Tudors & Stewarts 2015: A collection of 12 Profiles

Lady Margaret Beaufort

Mary I: Queen of England

James, Earl of Moray: Regent of Scotland

Jasper Tudor: Brother and Uncle of Kings

People

Who's Who in Britain's Bloody Crown

Who's Who in Wolf Hall

Politics & Economy

Field of Cloth of Gold

Succession: The Tudor Problem

The Pilgrimage of Grace and Exeter Conspiracy

Contents

Preface

Katharine of Aragon, Queen of England, was at the heart of politics in early sixteenth century Europe. She is one of the most famous of all England's Queens Consort and her battle to preserve her marriage has become the stuff of legend. But there was more to Katharine than the last ten years of her life. She was an exceptionally intelligent and learned woman, who played an influential role in the politics of the first part of Henry VIII's reign.

Katharine's story is, in many ways, a tragic one – her destiny was to act as a living symbol of the alliance between Spain and England and to provide an heir for England, which was only partially fulfilled. But for many years she was at the centre of European politics, Henry's loved and honoured wife.

The material was first published on www.tudortimes.co.uk

Family Tree

Katharine of Aragon
Queen of England

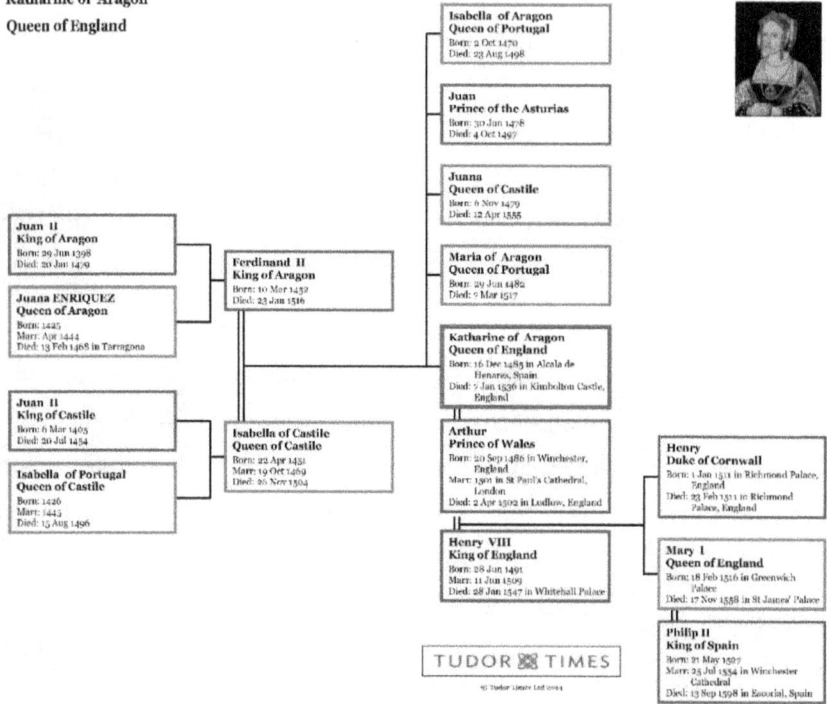

Isabella of Aragon
Queen of Portugal
Born: 2 Oct 1470
Died: 23 Aug 1498

Juan
Prince of the Asturias
Born: 30 Jun 1478
Died: 4 Oct 1497

Juana
Queen of Castile
Born: 6 Nov 1479
Died: 12 Apr 1555

Juan II
King of Aragon
Born: 29 Jun 1398
Died: 20 Jan 1479

Juana ENRIQUEZ
Queen of Aragon
Born: 1425
Marr: Apr 1444
Died: 13 Feb 1468 in Tarragona

Ferdinand II
King of Aragon
Born: 10 Mar 1452
Died: 23 Jan 1516

Maria of Aragon
Queen of Portugal
Born: 29 Jun 1482
Died: 7 Mar 1517

Katharine of Aragon
Queen of England
Born: 16 Dec 1485 in Alcala de
Henares, Spain
Died: 7 Jan 1536 in Kimbolton Castle,
England

Juan II
King of Castile
Born: 6 Mar 1405
Died: 20 Jul 1454

Isabella of Portugal
Queen of Castile
Born: 1428
Marr: 1447
Died: 15 Aug 1496

Isabella of Castile
Queen of Castile
Born: 22 Apr 1451
Marr: 19 Oct 1469
Died: 26 Nov 1504

Arthur
Prince of Wales
Born: 20 Sep 1486 in Winchester,
England
Marr: 1501 in St Paul's Cathedral,
London
Died: 2 Apr 1502 in Ludlow, England

Henry VIII
King of England
Born: 28 Jun 1491
Marr: 11 Jun 1509
Died: 28 Jan 1547 in Whitehall Palace

Henry
Duke of Cornwall
Born: 1 Jan 1511 in Richmond Palace,
England
Died: 22 Feb 1511 in Richmond
Palace, England

Mary I
Queen of England
Born: 18 Feb 1516 in Greenwich
Palace
Died: 17 Nov 1558 in St James' Palace

Philip II
King of Spain
Born: 21 May 1527
Marr: 25 Jul 1554 in Winchester
Cathedral
Died: 13 Sep 1598 in Escorial, Spain

TUDOR ☒ TIMES

© Tudor Times Ltd 2014

Part 1: Katharine of Aragon's Life Story

Chapter 1: Childhood

Katharine of Aragon was born in the small town of Alcala de Henares on the night of 15 - 16th December 1485, the fourth daughter and fifth surviving child of her parents, Ferdinand II of Aragon and Isabella I of Castile. Some six years previously Isabella had confirmed her hold on the kingdom of Castile by defeating the rival claimant Juana *'La Beltranaja'* and her marriage to Ferdinand, who became King of Aragon in that same year of 1479, had combined all Spain under their sovereignty, although the kingdoms remained as separate states.

A few days after her birth, dressed in a christening gown of white brocade lined with green velvet and a gold lace trim, Katharine was baptised by the Bishop of Palencia. At the time of Katharine's birth her parents were engaged in a war and the first five or so years of her life were spent following the army Ferdinand and Isabella were leading to fulfil their ambition to complete the Christian Reconquista of Spain.

For centuries after the Iberian Peninsula was overrun by the Moors in 711 AD, the Christian Kingdoms had fought back, until, inch by inch, the Moors had been driven into the last stronghold, the Kingdom of Granada on the south coast. The Spanish monarchs were determined that this final bastion would fall, and mounted a ten year campaign to win it. During this period, Isabella, accompanying the army (although not, of course, fighting) kept her children with her, to supervise their education.

In June 1491, Granada finally surrendered in a staged ceremony witnessed by Katharine and her siblings, but the royal family did not immediately take up residence there – instead they continued to travel around Spain, as the Catholic Kings (a title granted to Ferdinand and Isabella by the Pope after the fall of Granada) toured their kingdoms, administering justice and asserting royal authority. In around 1499, a more permanent Court was established in the Alhambra, the jewel of Granada, one of the most sophisticated and elegant palaces in the whole of Europe.

Katharine and her siblings received the best education available in the 1490s. Queen Isabella was determined that her daughters would be better educated than she had been, and had them taught Latin, the language of diplomacy, normally only taught to boys. Katharine wrote and spoke it fluently. She also studied the other branches of an early Humanist education – history, poetry, the writings of Aristotle and other philosophers and law. In addition, she learnt the traditional skills of upper class women – managing a great household, needlework, both plain and fine, music, dancing, etiquette, pastimes including chess, tables, cards, and hunting.

A key element of Katharine's education was, of course, the practice of her religion. Isabella was famously devout and her daughters were brought up to consider their faith the most important thing in life.

The purpose of Katharine's education was to make her a suitable wife for her future husband, and to give her enough knowledge and wisdom to influence him to think favourably of her native country. Royal women were the living symbol of alliances between their native land and their husband's realm.

Having completed the conquest of the Moorish Kingdom, Ferdinand had turned his not inconsiderable talents as a military strategist and soldier to the recovery of Pyrenean provinces lost by Aragon to France, and to the increase of his holdings in Southern Italy.

The rivalry for the dominance of Italy by France and Spain was the foremost European political problem in the first half of the 16th century and the relative strength of the contending parties at different times is the backdrop to the whole of Katharine's life. The Kings of France, first Charles VIII, then Louis XII and finally François I, were determined to make good their claim to the Duchy of Milan. At the same time Ferdinand wished to dominate not only the island of Sicily, which had been ruled by the Crown of Aragon since 1282, but also to regain the mainland kingdom of Naples which had devolved upon his illegitimate uncle, Ferrante, in 1458, once Ferrante died in 1494. Caught between the two powers, was the papacy, which ruled over central belt of the peninsula, known as the Papal States, although the extent of these fluctuated.

Chapter 2: Alliances

Ferdinand and Isabella's strategy was political as well as military. They planned a series of marriages for their children which sought to isolate France politically. The most important alliance of all was with Portugal. It shared a border with Castile and also sheltered Isabella's former rival for the throne in a Portuguese convent, so, peace had to be maintained. This was achieved first through the marriage of Ferdinand and Isabella's oldest daughter, also named Isabella, to Crown Prince Alfonso, then, following his death, to his cousin, Manuel.

The next element of the plan was a brilliant double alliance with the House of Hapsburg. The Holy Roman Emperor elect (he was never actually crowned) Maximilian II had two children – Philip the Fair, who had inherited the duchy of Burgundy from his mother, Mary, and

Marguerite of Austria. These two siblings were paired with Katharine's brother Juan, and sister, Juana. This meant that France would be entirely surrounded by hostile forces.

Katharine's own future was decided when she was around four years old. In the Treaty of Medina del Campo of 14th November 1489, her parents promised her to Arthur, Prince of Wales, son of Henry VII of England. This match was rather more of a gamble for Katharine's parents in that the Tudor dynasty was not well established in England in 1489 and there was the possibility that Henry VII might be deposed. Nevertheless Ferdinand and Isabella were sufficiently impressed by the English King to enter into the betrothal. The plan was for Katharine to travel to England when she reached the age of 14.

When Katharine was 10 her sister Juana sailed for Burgundy. The fleet which had delivered her returned to Spain carrying Marguerite of Austria, Juan's bride. On 18 March 1497 in the city of Burgos in northern Castile, Marguerite was presented to the Spanish court. Katharine, wearing a gown of brocaded cloth of gold together with a crimson scarf and a black mantilla, was in attendance, together with her sisters, the recently widowed Isabella, and Maria. The influence that the marriage of Juan and Marguerite may have had on Katharine should not be overlooked in considering her later life.

The young couple were aged about seventeen and were so infatuated with each other that Juan's doctors warned him to restrain his physical passions. His sudden, premature death, after only six months of marriage, was diagnosed as '*overexertion in the marital bed.*'

Ferdinand and Isabella were devastated personally and politically. A further blow fell when Marguerite miscarried a male foetus. With no child to keep her in Spain, Marguerite returned to her father in Burgundy but she had struck up an enduring friendship with Katharine, which became important later when Marguerite acted as Regent of the Low Countries for Charles, son of Philip and Juana.

In some ways Katharine's childhood was physically demanding – the peripatetic Spanish court travelled far and wide across the kingdoms – accommodation was in inns or abbeys, provisions were not always easy to find and the language and customs of the different sub kingdoms varied widely. The Royal household packed its belongings so frequently that Katharine and her sister Maria regularly had their own mules for carrying their gear. Of the 16 Christmases of Katharine's childhood, 13 were spent in different cities. Her parents were as loving and attentive as it was possible for monarchs to be – there are records of Ferdinand buying dolls for his daughter and the children were kept close.

Whilst the Spanish court was very formal in its manners, with men and women largely segregated, dancing and music were popular pastimes and Queen Isabella's library of chivalric romances included tales of King Arthur and his knights and the Spanish tale of chivalry, Tirant Lo Blanc.

Personal hygiene was so highly prized that at Isabella's court, she and her daughters bathed and washed their hair more frequently than was perhaps the norm in Europe.

Ferdinand and Isabella were determined to show their power and authority across the land and part of this involved the imposition of a strict Catholic culture. Mediaeval Spain had accepted the coexistence of the Christian Jewish and Muslim faiths. In 1492 the Jews were expelled from Spain and Catholic orthodoxy imposed with the introduction of the Inquisition. On the positive side, the Spanish church was reformed to remove many of the abuses that were apparent in the rest of Europe.

Chapter 3: Wife

In accordance with the Treaty of Medina del Campo, Katharine was to be sent to England as soon as practicable after her fourteenth birthday, and, in the meantime, had been married to Arthur by proxy. A number of letters survive from the 1490s, between the Spanish Kings and the King and Queen of England. Queen Elizabeth of York wrote on several occasions to Queen Isabella, asking after her health and that of Katharine, and suggesting that Katharine should learn to speak French.

Katharine's biographer, Patrick Williams, has speculated that this request implies that Elizabeth thought Katharine did not have a high linguistic ability and would not be able to learn English. It is perhaps more likely that the request was made because French was the language in most common use at Henry VII's court. As it happened, Katharine was not formally taught either French or English, and the extant letters she and Arthur wrote to each other during the period of their betrothal are in Latin.

By the summer of 1499 Katharine's family had been decimated. The deaths of Juan and his wife's fœtus had been followed by the death of Princess Isabella, and then that of her two-year-old son, Miguel. The Infanta Maria was sent to Portugal to replace her sister and Katharine was left as the last child at home. The time was drawing near for her to set out for England, but her parents prevaricated. Ferdinand seems to have been at least as concerned about having to send his daughter's enormous dowry as the girl herself, whilst Isabella clearly did not want to part with her child.

Court life became more sombre, but at least Katharine had the beauty of the Alhambra, where the royal household had finally settled, to console her. The symbol of the Kingdom of Granada, the pomegranate (a play on the words pomme (apple) de Granada) became one of her most widely used personal badges.

But Katharine's marriage could not be postponed forever. Back in England Henry was content with some delay – it appears that he was concerned over his son's health and did not wish him to enter married life too young. Postponement till 1501 was agreed on by both sides, but eventually the day came and on 21st May 1501 Katharine set out from the Alhambra on her long journey north.

It took the Princess' entourage, headed by her very strict governess (or duenna), Doña Elvira Manuel, and Doña Elvira's husband, Pedro Manrique, nearly 3 months to reach the north coast. The party finally set sail from Spain in late September 1501. After appalling storms, they landed at Plymouth on 2nd October. The entourage made its way in slows stages towards London, being intercepted at Dogmersfield in Hampshire, by Henry and Arthur.

Despite the objections of Doña Elvira to Katharine being seen by her new family before her wedding day, the King demanded to see her. Katharine acquiesced gracefully, and entertained the company by dancing in Spanish fashion.

Arthur and Katharine's wedding took place on 14th November, 1501, at St Paul's Cathedral amidst sumptuous pageantry and ceremony. The bride was led to the altar by the ten-year-old boy who was about to become her brother-in-law, Henry, Duke of York. Arthur was six weeks past his fifteenth birthday.

Following the ceremony, the Court returned to the Palace of Westminster to continue festivities and to witness the ceremonial bedding of the couple. What happened next was to be the subject of much discussion at a later date.

In early 1502, the question arose as to whether Katharine should be allowed to accompany Arthur back to Ludlow, his seat in the Marches of Wales, where he exercised his role as Prince of Wales and head of the Council of Wales and the Marches. There were concerns about the health of the couple, as too much sexual activity between young people was considered dangerous – the example of Katharine's brother was not far to seek. In the event, it was decided that she would go with him, and accompanied by her new English ladies, and Arthur's household, they set out for Wales.

At this time, Katharine began a friendship with Margaret Plantagenet, later Countess of Salisbury, that would last for the rest of Katharine's life. Margaret was the first cousin of Queen Elizabeth of York, and around fifteen years older than Katharine. She and her husband, Sir Richard Pole, were members of Arthur's entourage.

The young Prince and Princess of Wales arrived in Ludlow in December of 1501. He was learning to be a king, and she was adjusting to a new country, three new languages (the French of the Court, the English of everyday speech in the household, and the Welsh of the borders), new food, and, probably most noticeably, new, and not very charming, weather. The contrast between the fierce heat and equally fierce cold of Spain, and the soft, damp, cool weather of the Welsh Marches must have been stark.

Whatever the state of their physical relationship, Katharine and Arthur were not able to enjoy married life for long. By 2nd April, Arthur was dead – possibly of sweating sickness, perhaps of tuberculosis, testicular cancer or even from influenza. The latter may be a possibility as Katharine herself was ill for many weeks.

Chapter 4: Widow

Arthur was buried in Tewkesbury Abbey, where the last Lancastrian Prince of Wales was also interred. Katharine set out for London in a litter, draped in black, sent by Queen Elizabeth. Initially, no-one was quite sure what to do with the young widow, or with her brother-in-law. If Katharine were pregnant, her child would take precedence, so some time had to be left before Henry was proclaimed as Prince of Wales. In due course, it became apparent that Arthur had not left an heir – surprisingly, what he did leave, was a will giving all his possessions to his sister Margaret, betrothed to James IV of Scotland.

Although Queen Isabella's immediate reaction had been to request the return of her daughter, Henry and Ferdinand had other ideas. Both kings were parsimonious and disinclined to give up a bargain, and they now fell out about money. Katharine had been allowed to bring part of her dowry in jewels and household goods, with some cash up front, and the remainder to be paid in instalments. In return for her dowry, Katharine was to receive a jointure of a third of the revenues of the Prince of Wales, in the event of her widowhood.

If Katharine were to be returned to Spain, Henry would have to pay her jointure, but as he had not received her dowry, that did not seem like a good deal. In addition, the alliance between the two countries was still valuable. It was decided therefore, that Katharine would be betrothed to Henry, now Prince of Wales, and that they would be married when he reached the age of fifteen. The remainder of Katharine's dowry was to be paid, and King Henry would support her and her household.

There was another bit of administration to be attended to, as well. Because Katharine had been married to his brother, there was considered to be a bond of either consanguinity (if the marriage had been consummated) or of affinity, (if it had not) between her and Henry. Such a bond was a barrier to matrimony, and would require a Papal Dispensation to remove it. Such dispensations were frequent, and not considered controversial, however, it was important that they covered the details of the case in point.

The correct wording of the document depended on which type of bond existed. No-one seemed quite sure what Katharine and Arthur's relationship had been. Her duenna said that the marriage had not been consummated, but her confessor thought it had. In the event, a dispensation was granted on the basis that the marriage had been consummated, but a second version appears to have been issued as a Papal Brief, permitting the marriage 'even if the marriage had PERHAPS been consummated'. A letter from King Ferdinand states that it was well-known that the marriage had NOT been consummated, but he was going for the belt and braces approach, lest the slippery English try to wriggle out of the deal – not that Ferdinand's word should be taken to stand for much, as will become clear later.

For the next seven years, Katharine's existence was pretty miserable. In February 1503, her mother-in-law died, following which King Henry became more parsimonious and suspicious of Yorkist plots. Her own mother died in 1504, which was a great grief to her, and significantly lessened her value in King Henry's eyes, as Isabella's crown went to Juana and her husband, Philip, leaving Ferdinand to rule over a much diminished territory. Practical life was difficult too. She was kept very short of money by her father-in-law, her father failed to pay over her dowry, and she was reduced to selling her plate to buy food. Within her household, civil war broke out between her duenna and her confessor, and she was seldom allowed to see her betrothed or spend time at Court.

Katharine took refuge in her religion, and began to practice a level of austerity that prompted a letter from King Henry to the Pope, asking him to give Katharine's betrothed the authority to forbid her from indulging in excessive fasting and praying. His Holiness duly obliged, and Prince Henry received the information that his affianced wife's body was not her own to control, but must be subordinated to his authority so as to prevent her doing anything that might inhibit childbearing.

This was followed by a scandal relating to her new confessor. He was young, attractive, not as celibate as he ought to have been, and was considered to have far too much influence over her. She absolutely refused to dismiss him, writing to her father that he was the best confessor a woman in her position could have.

The arguments in the Princess' household between her servants and the various ambassadors of Spain who tried to talk King Henry into fulfilling the marriage treaty with Prince Henry became almost farcical, as the factions in Spain, between Castile and Aragon, were played out in microcosm in Katharine's household.

In 1507, her political position improved when she herself received letters of accreditation as Ambassador. Katharine showed a talent for intrigue and political machination that stood her in good stead in later life. In particular she played upon Henry VII's desire to marry her now widowed sister, the Queen of Castile, as a way of encouraging him to look favourably on her own marriage to the Duke of York. She learned to communicate in code and translate replies. All this gave her a new lease of life and energy, but after an initial improvement in her status, her father's failure to send the remainder of the dowry gave Henry VII a continued excuse to prevaricate over the marriage. In part her value was diminished by the arrangement that Henry made for her nephew, Charles, to marry his daughter, Mary, in a treaty agreed in 1507.

Chapter 5: Queen of England

On 21st April 1509, Henry VII died. Katharine, together with her sister-in-law Mary, called the Princess of Castile in recognition of her betrothal to Charles, were issued with appropriate mourning garb and horses to take part in the funeral procession. Within days the new king, Henry VIII, declared his intention of marrying Katharine and the ceremony took place on 11th June at the Palace of Placentia (Greenwich Palace) where Henry had been born. Ferdinand appeared to have no problem coming up with the money for the dowry once he was assured that the marriage would take place. Henry and Katharine were crowned together on 24th June 1509 and Katharine, triumphant in white satin with her much admired auburn hair hanging loose, was transformed from a widow, living on money from pawning her jewels and plate, to a Queen.

The newly married couple threw themselves into the pleasures of power and married life. They hunted, danced, enjoyed music and spent as much time as they could together. They appeared to onlookers to be deeply in love and both sent affectionate letters to her father saying how happy they were. Ferdinand responded by sending Henry some expensive Spanish horses that Katharine had requested.

The internal affairs of Spain affected England to a certain degree. The Queen of Castile, Katharine's sister, Juana, was deemed, rightly or wrongly, to be incapable of ruling. Her heir was Charles, Archduke of Austria, Duke of Burgundy and paternal grandson of the Emperor Maximilian. Charles' other grandfather, Ferdinand, had no intention of letting the Burgundian interest hold sway in Castile, which he was ruling on his daughter's behalf. He was therefore reluctant to approve Charles's betrothal to Henry VIII's sister, Mary, and was still hoping to have a son of his own by his second wife, Germaine de Foix, to inherit Aragon. Henry, in a letter of July 1509 announcing the happy news of Katharine's pregnancy, agreed with Ferdinand that Maximilian's and Charles' desertion of their old alliance with Spain and England was a retrograde step. Nevertheless there was no move to break the betrothal between Charles and Mary.

Later in the year, Ferdinand was pleased to hear that Henry was considering allying with Ferdinand himself, Maximilian and Charles against the French, to preserve the independence of Venice which Louis XII was threatening. He counselled against immediate war with France, affirming that so long as he himself lived the French would not dare to attack England, but warned that the French were likely to provoke trouble in Scotland.

A month or so later Ferdinand seemed to be ready to join an alliance against France. This was music to Henry's ears and preparations began to be made for an attack on the old enemy. Katharine was delighted that her husband and father appeared to be of one mind.

There is only one report of dissension between the King and Queen in their first year of marriage: a rumour arose at court that Lady Anne Hastings, the sister both of the Duke of Buckingham (a man with a substantial claim to the throne) and one of Katharine's ladies in waiting, Lady Elizabeth Stafford, was having an affair with a gentleman of Henry's bed chamber, Sir William Compton. Before long, it got about that Compton was just a front for the real lover, Henry himself. Lady Anne was packed off by her husband to a convent and Lady Elizabeth was dismissed by Henry for causing trouble.

Katharine's anger and jealousy was severe enough for it to be reported in foreign dispatches. Whether Henry was really the guilty party is unclear – given his general romantic streak and genuine love for Katharine it seems unlikely that he strayed so early. This view might also be supported by the fact that in 1528, when Compton died, he left a considerable bequest to Lady Anne.

Chapter 6: Henry, Duke of Cornwall

On the last day of January 1510, Katharine felt a pain in her leg, went into labour, and miscarried. Her physicians assured her that she was still pregnant, based presumably, on the fact that her womb remain swollen. She even formally '*took her chamber*' in March and orders were given for the accoutrements she would need for childbed and for dressing an infant.

At the time, Luis Caroz, Ferdinand's ambassador, suggested that the Queen had never been pregnant at all but that she was suffering from a phantom pregnancy. He based this on the information that he had received that she was still menstruating. The whole matter is deeply confusing as it was not until May that she announced to her father that she had '*recently*' given birth to a stillborn daughter. Since the Queen continued with the information that, whilst in labour, she had vowed to send a gift to the shrine of Saint Peter Martyr, it doesn't seem likely that there was no pregnancy at all.

Much has been written about this reticence with the truth and indeed Dr David Starkey uses Katharine's lack of truthfulness here as a proof that she lied about the consummation of her marriage to Arthur. In Katharine's defence it might be pointed out that her mother had miscarried one fœtus in a twin pregnancy but carried the other to term. Katharine may well have believed that the same was the case with her –

and perhaps it was. We cannot know the intimate details of exactly what happened - a single miscarriage, a phantom pregnancy or two miscarriages.

The Queen was obviously in good enough health to engage in marital relations with her husband as, given the date of her next confinement, she must have fallen pregnant again in early April 1510.

This time the pregnancy proceeded smoothly, with Katharine spending much of her time at Eltham Palace, and in December 1510 she *'took her chamber'*, the ceremonial withdrawal in preparation for childbed that was laid down by her husband's grandmother, Lady Margaret Beaufort, in her rules for royal conduct.

The birth took place at Richmond on 1st January 1511. To the joy of both parents, Katharine bore a son, who was immediately named as Duke of Cornwall. The exultant father hurried to the shrine of the Virgin Mary at Walsingham in Norfolk to give thanks. As soon as Katharine was churched, 40 days after the birth, the Royal couple left Richmond, leaving Prince Henry in the safety of his nursery, whilst they undertook the journey back to Westminster.

Young Henry's birth was greeted with rapture and joyous celebrations, culminating in a great joust. This joust was the most extravagant of Henry's whole reign. The King's armour was engraved with intertwined 'H's and 'K's and he jousted under the name of *'Cœur Loyale'*, Sir Loyal Heart.

Sadly, in a tragedy that was both personal and political, baby Henry died at eight weeks old. Katharine was distraught. Henry, too, was grieved but he made every effort to comfort his wife: after all infant deaths were not uncommon and Katharine had been pregnant twice within two years of marriage, so it was not unreasonable to believe that the next time that they would be lucky. Fortunately for the couple, their mutual affection was not purely based in their need for children. Katharine, although she had no official political role, was extremely influential in these years and was still acting as Ferdinand's chief envoy.

Chapter 7: A Year of Conflict

One of the political areas in which the King and Queen were as one, was in their desire to regain the English territories in France. As the dismemberment of France, or at least the regaining of the kingdom of Navarre, which the French had encroached upon, was also Spanish policy, the two countries could ally against Louis XII.

It is probable that Katharine and Henry genuinely believed that Spanish and English interests were the same, but that was a naive position. Ferdinand cared little about Henry's claim to be King of France and was very much more interested in his own Italian and Navarrese ambitions. Ferdinand was no seeker after military glory for its own sake – he had achieved that with the conquest of Granada. What he wanted was territorial domination in Italy and Navarre, and he would use war or peace, truth or lies, loyalty or betrayal, to achieve it.

Whatever Katharine and Henry's jingoistic ambitions, the King's councillors, many of whom had served his more cautious father, wish to dissuade him from war, and in the event it was not until 1512 that Henry first sent an army abroad. Under the leadership of Thomas Grey, Marquess of Dorset, Henry's maternal cousin, a force of 6,000 landed in Spain with the object of joining Ferdinand's army and the combined force invading Aquitaine. Ferdinand used their presence to mount a surprise attack on Navarre. Henry's men were poorly provisioned, badly trained and, unable to carry out their mission of invading Aquitaine, took to looting and molesting the local Spaniards. Eventually, running out of supplies and close to starvation, they were obliged to return home.

Ferdinand declared that the whole fiasco had been the fault of Dorset and his men although some of Henry's councillors, unsurprisingly, believed that Ferdinand had deliberately used the arrival of English troops to cover his own actions.

Henry and Katharine chose to accept Ferdinand's explanation, but from this point forward Katharine seems to have understood that her father's and her husband's interests were not always consistent. In her mind there was no contest between the two and she would always put Henry's interests first. Nevertheless, Henry was determined on war with France on his own account and the Queen was in absolute agreement with his ambitions.

As Henry began to prepare for war in earnest, Katharine became deeply involved in the planning stages. Queen Isabella had acted as quartermaster for her army in the re-conquest of Granada and Katharine showed a similar interest in the details of military planning. She and Henry had a shared interest in the navy – whilst the largest ship afloat in Europe was the 'Michael', owned by Henry VIII's brother-in-law, James IV of Scotland, Henry had commissioned new ships including the 'Peter Pomegranate' – named to reflect Katharine's personal badge of the pomegranate. According to the Venetian reports, Katharine was trying to persuade Henry to build four galleasses – a type of warship.

The English began to attack French shipping in early 1513, but the campaign was a disaster, resulting in the death of Sir Thomas Knyvet, one of Henry and Katharine's favourite courtiers, and also Lord Edward Howard, son of the Earl of Surrey and a friend of the royal couple.

By the summer of 1513, England and France were at war. Henry was determined to lead his troops himself and set sail from Dover in June.

Before he left he appointed Katharine as Queen Governor or Regent of England. She was to have full regal powers with the exception of the appointment of bishops. Most importantly, she had authority to raise an army and to distribute money from the Treasury. Henry declared his faith in his wife by lauding her '*honour, excellence, prudence forethought and faithfulness*'.

Although a large portion of Henry's nobles had accompanied him to France, Katharine did retain the services of a council, including Thomas Howard, Earl of Surrey. Surrey had been Henry's uncle by marriage, married to Anne of York, and was considered one of the most able military commanders in England. He had many years of experience in both negotiating with Scotland and containing the persistent low-level warfare that troubled the Anglo-Scots border.

Surrey's experience in the North was vital as the action that Scotland would take in the event of an Anglo-French war was uncertain. England and Scotland had been bound by the Treaty of Perpetual Peace which had been signed at the turn of the century, and fulfilled with the marriage of Henry's sister, Margaret, to the King of Scots. But Scotland had also had an alliance with France for a much longer period and the two agreements now conflicted. King James, although he tried to mediate between the parties, was forced to choose. Eventually, he felt unable to deny the Auld Alliance with France.

Henry's allies were rather more powerful than Louis': most importantly the Pope, who was offended by Louis' threats to call a General Council of the Church at Pisa; the Emperor Maximilian and, at least on paper, Ferdinand, although it was not long before Ferdinand once again showed his true colours by making a truce with France. Henry was incandescent with rage, but pressed on.

Back home, Katharine was busy with her duties as Regent, although this did not prevent her taking an interest in Henry's health and writing frequently to Thomas Wolsey, who was managing the logistical arrangements, asking him to ensure that Henry did not catch a cold. There exist quantities of administrative papers – patents, grants, writs et cetera – signed by 'Katharine, Queen of England'.

It was soon a more urgent matter to be dealt with. As anticipated, James IV made the decision to invade in support of the French. Katharine had been proactive in beginning to raise troops in July when it was first reported that James IV was gathering an army. Although in her letters Katharine referred to her preparations for war in suitably modest feminine style by saying she was 'horribly busy preparing banners' in fact she was taking rather more vigorous actions, despatching the *Mary Rose* at the channel and ordering food military supplies and armour to be shipped north as well as reinforcements for the Army that Surrey was raising in the northern counties. The Queen herself sent out orders for further troops to gather in the Midlands and sent out letters to the southern counties to begin preparations. Scots living in England were to be banished.

Meanwhile Henry had had some success in his campaign – including capturing the Duke of Longueville, who was sent to Katharine as a hostage. She felt the Duke's presence to be rather an encumbrance as she intended to travel north with her army so she sent him to the Tower of London (the palace part, rather than the prison) to keep him out of the way.

In early September the Queen rode north to confront the enemy. She was accompanied by a herald and pursuivant (a junior herald used for sending messages, particularly for declaring war.) She also had six trumpeters, a necessary accoutrement for an army. The banners of

England and Spain, as well as of St George and the Virgin fluttered in the air as she made her way through the countryside.

It is not hard to imagine Katharine remembering the campaigns of her childhood as the Spanish royal family followed the army in its conquest of Granada. As a woman she would not, of course, be in the ranks of the troops, but she did order armoured headgear, presumably with the view of being at least in the vicinity of any battle. Some sources say that Katharine addressed the troops directly, urging them to be ready to defend their territory and reminding them that the courage of the English 'excelled that of all other nations'.

Before Katharine had got further north than Buckingham, in what was perhaps rather an anti-climax for her, news came that Surrey had won an overwhelming victory at the battle of Flodden. James IV had been killed and Scotland was now at England's mercy.

Katharine was overjoyed by the news and delighted to receive evidence of James's death in the dispatch to her of his bloodstained coat – that is the cloth tabard showing his arms he had worn over his armour. She sent a triumphant letter to Henry glorying in the destruction of the enemy.

'This battle hath been to Your Grace and all your realm the greatest honour that could be and more than you should win all the Crown of France (it may be that Henry did not appreciate that sentence!) Your Grace shall see how I can keep my promise, sending you for your banners a King's coat.'

She added that she would have liked to have sent James's body but 'our Englishman's hearts would not suffer it.' This latter sentence has always been taken to mean that Katharine was rather blood-thirsty but the English were too soft-hearted to send the King's body abroad. Her triumphalism cannot be denied, but it could be interpreted to mean that Surrey and the others wish to keep the trophy themselves.

Katharine not surprisingly, urged Henry to give thanks to God for the victory and set out herself for Walsingham to show her gratitude at the shrine.

Once the first flush of victory was over, Katharine found it in her heart to pity her sister-in-law, the widowed Margaret, Queen of Scots, and sent her messages of consolation. The northern realm was devastated by the loss at Flodden but the English had neither the money nor the manpower to stage a full-scale conquest. A truce was agreed and Katharine was involved in the administration of paying the wages to the army and returning the artillery to the Tower and other locations.

In France, Henry had captured the towns of Therouanne and Tournai and defeated the French at the Battle of the Spurs. He had had the glory (and also the expense) of the Emperor himself fighting under him. Once again though, in the larger picture, Henry had been played for a fool. The towns he had captured were of little or no value to England but were extremely useful to the Emperor, forming a buffer zone between France and his own territories of Flanders.

Henry returned in October 1513 and had a joyful reunion with Katharine, who may have had a miscarriage during his absence.

Chapter 8: Disappointments

After Henry's return, the political landscape began to change. Ferdinand's health was deteriorating – the amount of attention paid to his young wife was one reason given, but their only child died at birth.

Ferdinand's heir was therefore either his daughter, Juana, or her son Charles. Ferdinand might have preferred his heir to be Juana's second son, Ferdinand, who had been brought up at the court of Aragon. Charles had been brought up in his late father's territory of Burgundy by his aunt, Marguerite of Austria (Katharine's sister-in-law), and Charles' other grandfather, the Emperor Maximilian, and was therefore essentially Hapsburg, rather than Spanish in outlook.

For Henry, the notion of Charles as King of both Spanish kingdoms was welcome. The prince had been betrothed to Henry's sister, Mary, since 1507 and in 1514 the time had come for the marriage to take place – this would reinforce England's links with both Spain, and its major trading partner, Burgundy.

Princess Mary was fitted out with all of the splendour that the match to a man who would probably be Emperor one day, required. She prepared to journey to Calais where her fiancé was to meet her for the wedding to take place in May. Archduchess Marguerite was pushing for the betrothal to be fulfilled but Maximilian and Charles (presumably on the former's instruction) were both dragging their feet. With a distinct lack of gallantry, 14-year-old Charles had been heard to complain that Mary, at 17, was old enough to be his mother!

Although Henry had continued his preparations for a further campaign in France throughout the winter of 1513 – 1514, when he heard in March that Maximilian and Ferdinand had signed a separate truce with Louis XII, he realised the extent of their duplicity.

With the continued prevarications of Maximilian and Charles over the wedding as a further goad, Henry, ably assisted by his minister, Thomas Wolsey, arranged a secret deal with Louis XII under which Princess Mary would be married to the ageing and gouty French King. Handily, the Duke of Longueville was still in England and able to act as proxy for his master in the ceremony. The Spanish ambassador was not invited to attend court and Katharine must have been heartily ashamed of her father. She was determined to act in every way as an English Queen and ceased correspondence with Ferdinand.

It is not clear to what extent Henry blamed Katharine for her father's behaviour but she undoubtedly came in for some of his anger and a Spanish observer suggested that the tragic outcome of her pregnancy that year (another still birth or early death of a son) was the result of grief caused by Henry's anger with her over her father's devious behaviour. Tempers cooled, and Henry remained, by and large, a loving husband, arranging a sumptuous masque for Christmas Day to entertain his grieving wife, but politically she was losing influence to Thomas Wolsey.

Katharine fell pregnant again in the spring of 1515 and it was perhaps soon after this that Henry began an affair with Elizabeth Blount. Bessie, as she is generally called, was a connection of Katharine's Lord Chamberlain, Lord Mountjoy. There was no question of Bessie being in any way a threat to Katharine's position. It was not uncommon for men, particularly kings, to have mistresses especially as marital relations were discouraged during pregnancy. Given Katharine's unhappy obstetric history it is likely that the couple avoided sex, lest it pose any risk to her condition.

It is unknown at what point Katharine became aware of Henry's affair. The Tudor court was rife with gossip, so she probably knew of it, but refrained from giving any public indication that she was concerned by it.

Although Katharine's political power was diminishing she was still taking an active interest in Henry's Navy. In October 1515 a new ship, 'Princess Mary', was launched, named for Henry's sister, the French Queen. Soon widowed after her marriage to Louis XII, Mary had returned to England, initially disgraced by her secret second marriage to

Henry's friend, Charles Brandon, Duke of Suffolk but now restored to her brother's favour. On the launching of the ship, Henry, Katharine and the French Queen dined on board. A second smaller barque was commissioned, finished in 1518 and named the *'Katherine Pleasaunce'*.

Chapter 9: Motherhood

In February 1516, Katharine finally held a healthy, live child in her arms. Her daughter, Mary, was born on the 18th of the month and christened a few days later at the Church of the Observant Friars, Greenwich. Unlike the Duke of Cornwall, Mary flourished. Katharine's immediate joy was somewhat alloyed by the news that her father had died in January, information which had been kept from her so as not to endanger the pregnancy.

The birth of a daughter was a positive outcome for Henry in that the baby was clearly healthy and likely to thrive. With his accustomed habit of accentuating the positive, Henry declared that both he and Katharine were young and boys would surely follow.

Royal mothers were not accustomed to undertaking physical care of their children and Katharine was no exception. Mary, being only a daughter, did not merit the independent household an oldest son would have been granted but had a small coterie of dedicated servants – nurses, rockers, serving women and a chaplain-cum-secretary. Mary was frequently with Henry and Katharine, who both took an intense interest in her, but the baby also spent considerable time in the quieter and healthier air of the small palace at Thames Ditton.

Although he still had no son, Henry now had an additional bargaining chip in European politics. With Ferdinand's death, Charles, Duke of Burgundy, had become King of Castile and Aragon in conjunction with his mother, Queen Juana. Juana remained confined for the rest of her life, allegedly mad, although the symptoms as described appear reminiscent of manic-depression rather than insanity.

In France, too, there was a new king, François I. Europe was now ruled by a triumvirate of young men. All three - Henry, Charles and François – sought military glory, which François had found in 1515 at his stunning victory at Marignano which brought the duchy of Milan into his hands.

For Charles, feats of arms would have to wait: the Spanish were unenthusiastic about their new king, who was disliked as a foreigner – he needed time, money, and friends to consolidate his kingship and to position himself to be elected as Emperor when Maximilian died. He was perhaps sorry that he had failed to marry Henry's sister when he had the opportunity, and alliance with England would be an important part of his policy for the first ten years of his reign.

For Henry, and of course Katharine, alliance with Charles was the preferred strategy. Charles' Burgundian territories had been England's most important trading partner for over a hundred years and any disturbance to the trade from war was damaging for both countries. But despite the constant desire to invade France, Henry was too short of money to indulge in a war. The result was that Henry and Wolsey looked to build an alliance with the newly powerful François through the betrothal of Katharine's daughter to the Dauphin in 1518. As well as monetary motives, Henry could comfort himself that he was acting as a true Christian in promoting the wider five-year truce proclaimed by Pope

Leo X, in the (futile) hope of uniting Christendom against the incursions of the Ottoman Empire.

The betrothal took place on 5th October and Mary, who was two and a half, acquitted herself well. Katharine was heavily pregnant, and must have been hoping against hope for a son. As part of the marriage negotiations, Henry had promised to recognise Mary as his heir if he had no son. The last thing Katharine would have wanted was her daughter carrying England into French hands. Alas, in November, Katharine bore another daughter who died either before or immediately after birth.

Of course, in 1518, neither Henry nor Katharine could have known that there would be no more pregnancies, and it appears that they still hoped for another six years. For Henry, there was the bitter-sweet arrival of his illegitimate son, Henry Fitzroy, in 1519 to prove that there was no reason why he should not have a son. In the meantime, Mary, although not formally acknowledged as Henry's heir, began to receive more attention.

In 1519, Charles of Spain was elected as Holy Roman Emperor. Both François and Henry had put their names forward, and the French king had spent a fortune on bribes, but to no avail. For Charles, the debt he incurred in obtaining an office which in actuality had no land or wealth attached to it made it something of a pyrrhic victory. Nevertheless, the prestige was enormous, and, for Katharine, the knowledge that her nephew was the secular leader of Christendom (in theory, if not in practice) must have added to her sense of the dignity of her own position.

Chapter 10: Diplomacy

The period 1520 -22 was, for Katharine, a time when she was again politically prominent, although in her role as Henry's consort and the embodiment of alliances, rather than in an active role as Regent. In 1520, Charles visited England en route between Spain and the Netherlands. He landed at Dover on 26th May and, following a lavish reception at Canterbury, had several private meetings with Henry and Katharine, although the substance of their discussions is not known. The trio also agreed to a second meeting to take place in the summer, after Henry and Katharine had finished their planned diplomatic visit to France.

A few days after Charles' departure, the English King and Queen sailed for Calais, to meet François I and his wife, Queen Claude, at the most magnificent public display of Henry's reign, the Field of Cloth of Gold. Katharine was treated with all possible honour by Henry – her suite of followers numbered 1,175 and she had her own lodgings and tents. Whilst the monarchs showed off to each other, Katharine and Claude seem to have struck up a genuine warmth.

Despite the elaborate and costly junketings of the meeting, it made little difference to political reality – Henry and Katharine left the meeting to travel to Gravelines, on the border with the Netherlands, where they met Charles and his aunt, Archduchess Marguerite. Katharine had not seen the Archduchess since she had left Spain, following the death of Juan, but we can imagine that they had a joyful reunion, and perhaps reminisced about the Spanish court of the 1490s.

At the meeting, it was agreed that the betrothal between Mary and the Dauphin would be broken off, and Mary would marry Charles when she reached the age of consent, in 1528. For the time being, the match was kept secret, but for Henry, the thought that his grandson might one day be Emperor was presumably some compensation for knowing that England would be absorbed into Charles' fiefdoms.

On 25th August 1521 a formal treaty was signed between Henry and Charles. It was not just a peace-time alliance – the signatories bound themselves to invade France in 1523, if Wolsey's efforts at reconciling François and Charles failed.

The treaty was extended in November to include the Kings of Portugal, Hungary and Denmark, ruled by Katharine's brother-in-law and the husbands of two of her nieces, respectively. Charles' power grew when his captain, Prospero Colonna, achieved a notable victory on 27th April 1522 at La Biococca, which reversed Francois' triumph at Marignano and gave Charles dominance in northern, as well as southern Europe.

Katharine could bask in her nephew's reflected glory, especially when he paid a second diplomatic visit to England in May 1522. The visit lasted six weeks and was a triumph of logistical organisation by Wolsey. Charles was accompanied by a large suite of nobles from his various territories as well as his administrative staff. Having travelled slowly from the coast, accompanied from Canterbury by Henry, Charles met Katharine and Mary at Greenwich on the evening of 2nd June where Katharine cried with delight, and Mary conceived a trust and affection for her cousin that would last for over thirty years.

Over the weeks of the visit, much attention was paid to the long history of alliance between England and Burgundy and Charles' own descent, like both Katharine and Henry, from John of Gaunt. The monarchs discussed the ins and outs of the preparations they would make for war with France and on 16th June Henry formally broke off his alliance with François on the pretext that the King of France had caused dissension within Christendom, preventing Europe from addressing the Ottoman menace.

The public treaty of 16th June was followed up by a private treaty which again confirmed the betrothal of Charles to Princess Mary. Their oldest son would inherit the throne of England, and with it, English claims (no matter how unrealistic) to the throne of France. There were also some financial arrangements whereby Charles would compensate Henry for the loss of the pensions and indemnities to the English Crown following previous wars with France. As Henry's ally and future son-in-law, Charles was then invested with the Order of the Garter.

It was all very well to promise war, but Henry did not have the money to deliver. The costs of the campaigns of 1512 and 1513 and Henry's extravagant lifestyle – not least the expenses of the Field of Cloth of Gold and the entertainment of Charles and his train for six weeks - had made serious inroads into the royal treasury. He was obliged to call Parliament to request funds. The Commons were unimpressed by Henry and Wolsey's demands and a very small sum was voted, to last for four years. In recognition of the financial limitations of both Henry and Charles it was agreed that the main invasion of France would be postponed until 1525. Nevertheless both parties would undertake some military action 1524 – Charles felt that he had done his part in various campaigns but that Henry failed to deliver on his promises.

Chapter 11: Storm Clouds

At some time during 1524 Henry seems to have stopped sleeping with Katharine. She was now 40 and had probably reached the menopause. There was no immediate question of this change in their personal life affecting Katharine's position as Queen but it did bring home to Henry that so long as they were married, he would have no legitimate sons.

Given the circumstances, Henry's arrangements for the future through the betrothal of Mary to Charles, appeared to be the best decision he could have make. This was reinforced on 24th February 1525 when Charles won the immensely important Battle of Pavia. François' forces were so overwhelmingly defeated that the King himself was taken hostage. Henry was overjoyed at hearing this and rushed to tell Katharine the good news. Relying on their treaties, he quickly sent emissaries to Charles with a view to planning how he himself might be crowned King of France or at the very least regain the old Angevin territories.

Charles, however, saw matters very differently. Believing that he had undertaken all the work and expense of defeating France, he was not inclined to share the spoils of victory with his uncle-by-marriage. He demanded that Mary be sent immediately to Spain in preparation for marriage, probably anticipating that Henry would not agree to send his heiress out of the kingdom unmarried. Unable to redeem himself with the Emperor, and unable to prosecute war in France himself as he had no money, Henry was obliged to come to terms with the French in the Treaty of The More of 30th August 1525.

Charles needed both money and men and he therefore decided that rather than waiting for Mary to grow up, he must marry immediately. Henry's refusal to send Mary to Spain gave him is escape route, and so he was free to marry their mutual cousin, Isabella of Portugal, who was not only of sufficient maturity to act as his Regent but also had a very attractive cash dowry. The agreement was made in October 1525 and the couple married the following March.

Katharine was now the symbol of an alliance which had gone disastrously wrong, and she was unable to redeem herself by the production of a male heir. Her new status as an encumbrance rather than a benefit was demonstrated as she was publicly humiliated in return for Henry's mortification at the hands of Charles.

Henry Fitzroy, the King's six-year-old son by Bessie Blount, was paraded at court and given the titles of Duke of Richmond and Somerset – significant titles in the House of Lancaster. He was also granted a grand household and given the role of Lieutenant-General of the north and it became apparent that Henry was at least considering having him legitimised in some way and declared his heir. At the same time, he had not completely abandoned the idea of Mary as his heir and she too was given a grand household and was sent to Ludlow to preside over the Council of Wales and the Marches, just as her uncle Arthur had done 30 years before.

Mary was not formally granted the title of Princess of Wales but it was used informally. Presumably, Katharine took this as an indication that her daughter would one day inherit the throne although parting with her nine-year-old child must have been a wrench. Over the three years that Mary spent in the Welsh Marches, she visited her parents at court on a number of occasions and she and Katharine corresponded regularly.

As well as political difficulties, there was soon a personal crisis to confront. By early 1526 Katharine must have heard the rumours that Henry had fallen in love with another woman - Anne Boleyn. Katharine had, of course, been aware of the Bessie Blount affair, but it is unclear if she ever knew of Henry's dalliance with Mary Boleyn. The new romance was to prove far more serious, although it is unlikely that in 1525/6 Henry was seriously contemplating replacing Katharine as Queen with Anne.

Chapter 12: Annulment

In early 1526 Henry began to question the validity of his marriage. Whilst the political background made the alliance with Spain less valuable than it had once been and personally Katharine was no longer sexually attractive to her husband, it would be unfair to Henry to suggest that he did not genuinely have concerns about the marriage.

Henry remained all his life a deeply religious man and if not quite such a splendid theological scholar as he deemed himself, certainly had a well-educated layman's knowledge of the Scriptures. It is very likely that, troubled by the lack of sons, he turned to his Bible for answers as to why God should be displeased with him. The fact that the answer he thought he found there also happened to be one that suited him personally and politically does not necessarily mean he was a hypocrite. In late 1526 he seems to have consulted with his Confessor on the topic.

In brief, Henry's argument was that marriage to his brother's widow was prohibited in the book of Leviticus, although Leviticus does not comment on whether the prohibition on sexual relationships with the brother's wife referred to a living or a dead brother. Henry chose not to opine on the book of Deuteronomy which positively required a man to marry his brother's widow.

The Catholic Church for centuries had forbidden such marriages, but Popes were frequently requested to grant dispensations which would permit otherwise banned unions. The argument in this case turned on Henry's suggestion that Pope Julius II could not have granted a valid dispensation in 1503, because it was not within his competence to dispense against a biblical law, as opposed to a church rule. This was a challenge to papal authority that was never going to play well in the early days of the Reformation but which many sincere Catholics could appreciate as a valid argument.

Popes had granted annulments to kings on far more dubious grounds in the past and, had the political situation being different, it is likely that Henry would have achieved his aim. Unfortunately for the King, during the period September 1526 to May 1527, Rome was overrun and comprehensively sacked by the unpaid troops of Charles V. The devastation and destruction wrought in the Holy City surpassed anything that had happened in Europe since the fall of the Roman Empire to the Goths.

Back in England, Cardinal Wolsey and Archbishop Warham of Canterbury set up a secret court to try the matter of the King's marriage. Katharine was not informed. For unknown reasons, Wolsey and Warham did not give a verdict but decided that the matter was too serious for them and must be settled by the Pope.

Pope Clement had far more pressing concerns on his mind – not least that his only hope of emerging from the Castel San Angelo where he was sheltering was dependent entirely on the goodwill of Charles. Upsetting Charles' aunt was not going to help his position – on the other hand, upsetting such a faithful son of the Church as Henry had been would limit Clement's ability to build a coalition that might rescue him from thraldom to the Emperor. These difficulties were compounded by Clement's own chronic indecisiveness.

On 22nd June 1527, Henry informed Katharine that he had become aware that their marriage was invalid and that they had lived in sin for 18 years. Katharine broke down into tears, but quickly riposted that as her marriage to Arthur had never been consummated, she had never actually been his wife and therefore the Levitical prohibition did not apply.

That this speedy response was made suggests that she had previously been warned of what was happening and had prepared her arguments. She also had sufficient presence of mind to send a messenger to the Emperor to warn him of events in England.

Charles responded by asking the Pope to revoke Wolsey's position as Legate a Latere and also requested that Henry should desist from his attempts to have the marriage annulled. Throughout the years that followed, Charles gave verbal support to Katharine but there was never any real possibility of him intervening in any military way – he had neither the money nor the men to open yet another front of war. He did not even apply trade sanctions – a ban on trade with Burgundy might have encouraged Katharine's supporters in England (who were legion) to resist Henry.

For two years the argument was batted backwards and forwards with little progress until in May 1529 a second cardinal, Lorenzo Campeggio, arrived from Rome to make a public trial of the case.

Henry and Wolsey had requested Clement to give the two cardinals sufficient power to make a binding decision. Clement, desperate to retain Henry's support but menaced by the very much more proximate Charles, gave Campeggio the required decretal brief (which allows the court to make a decree that is binding) but forbade him from using it.

Chapter 13: Court Drama

Before the trial, which was held at Blackfriars, opened, Cardinal Campeggio made a last-ditch attempt to resolve the problem through persuading Katharine to enter a convent. Katharine completely rejected such a solution unless Henry were also willing to enter a monastery. Katharine is not someone who strikes the modern reader as a humorous woman, but clearly she had her moments. She also refused to recognise that the court could give a binding judgement and affirmed that she would not accept a verdict other than one given by the Pope himself.

To support her arguments, Katharine also produced a copy of a brief issued by Julius II in 1504. This expanded on the original dispensation, taking into account the possibility that Katharine's marriage to Arthur had not been consummated. Thus from Katharine's perspective, the dispensation was valid in any circumstance if the Pope had the power to dispense Levitical law, but if he had not such power, no dispensation was in fact necessary since, she said, she and Arthur had not consummated their marriage.

The court opened on 31st May 1529. The first two weeks were taken up with administration (legal delays are nothing new!). Katharine appeared in front of Cardinals and informed them that as they had both received benefits at the hands of the King, they could not be impartial. She wanted her case to be judged by an unbiased court. Unsurprisingly the Cardinals paid no attention to her objection and summoned both King and Queen to appear before them on 28th June.

Katharine had been appointed lawyers and churchmen to argue her case, including John Fisher, Bishop of Rochester, who was her most vociferous supporter throughout the whole case. She was also allowed Flemish lawyers. Warham, Archbishop of Canterbury, who had performed both her marriage ceremony and her coronation, was an unenthusiastic opponent of Henry's plan.

On being called, Henry explained to the court his doubts about his matrimony and requested that the Cardinals resolve the case promptly. Then, to the astonishment of the court, Katharine stood up and, in a gesture which has gone down in history, crossed the court room floor and knelt in front of her husband. She gave an impassioned speech in which she pleaded with him to dismiss the case, reiterated her devotion to him as a wife and pointed out that they had had many children together even though it had not been God's will that they should live. She swore again that she had been a virgin at their marriage and finally she requested that if the case were not stopped she could have time to consult with her family in Spain.

Henry remained unresponsive, so she left the court, refusing all calls to return. Over the next few days the Cardinals and Henry's other bishops pleaded with Katharine to relent and cease to contest the matter but she adamantly refused.

Meanwhile, in Europe, Charles and François had come to an accommodation. This increased Clement VII's need to appease Charles and, as requested by Katharine, the case was revoked to Rome. He sent a letter of justification to Henry pointing out that although he himself did not believe that the judges were biased, since Katharine patently did fear prejudice he, Clement, had no choice but to accept her request.

This failure of the legatine court presaged the end of Cardinal Wolsey's influence. Katharine had long blamed him for the annulment proceedings but after his departure in disgrace matters proceeded. Wolsey was never the driving force behind Henry's desire to dissolve his marriage – it was always Henry himself, with the added fillip of Anne Boleyn's urging.

Just as Henry was banishing his most experienced and talented minister, who might well have been able to obtain the annulment had his advice been followed at the beginning, Katharine found a new supporter – Eustace Chapuys, the Imperial ambassador, who arrived in London in September 1529.

Katharine was becoming increasingly suspicious that Henry's motives were not entirely pure – although Anne Boleyn had been sent away from the Royal court during the period of the court hearing so as not to give the wrong impression to Campeggio, she was now back at Henry's side and was acting as Queen in waiting.

Meanwhile Clement's hands were further tied as Charles made a triumphal progress through Italy to be crowned as Holy Roman Emperor. The Pope received something in return for the miseries of the sack of Rome – the Medici family were restored to power in Florence. In March 1530 Clement inched towards making progress in the case, but not to a level to satisfy either party. He made no judgement but instead drafted a Papal Bull commanding Henry not to contemplate remarriage until the matter of his marriage to Katharine had been definitively settled. In the meantime, she was to be treated as his lawful wife. To ensure that Henry was aware of the Bull and that a refusal to permit it to enter England could not be used to claim ignorance, the Bull was to be posted on the church doors in Rome and also in Dunkirk, Bruges, Tournai and Therouanne. This draft was followed up by a prohibition on any publications condemning the marriage until he made his judgement.

Chapter 14: Banished

Still reluctant to displease Henry, the Bulls were not published, but Clement had achieved the feat of angering both Henry and Katharine. Incensed by his failure to order Henry to treat her as his wife, she sent Clement a letter clearly laying out what she conceived to be his duty to her. She pleaded with him to cease delaying and to judge the case.

In her letter to Clement, Katharine reiterates her belief that Henry himself is not responsible for the aspersions cast on their marriage but blames it all on his advisers. It is hard to know whether Katharine was sincere in this belief. She would not be the first or the last wronged wife to blame anybody but her husband and perhaps she still believed that if their married life were to be resumed it would be better for her to think well of him. It is hard to doubt that Katharine's view of Henry as lacking agency must have been deeply irritating to a king who believed himself supreme.

Perhaps Katharine's beliefs were not entirely unrealistic, as in the summer of 1530 she and her husband still presided over the court together and treated each other politely and respectfully in public, and both spent time with their daughter, Mary. Katharine was also allowed to see Chapuys, who never ceased badgering Charles to do more for his aunt.

By January of the following year, however, Anne Boleyn was more prominent than ever – to the extent that the Pope wrote to Henry pointing out that his behaviour was scandalous. Anne was growing in confidence and although she still referred to Katharine as Queen said that she would rather see her hanged than acknowledge her as mistress.

The pressure began to tell on Katharine's health and she was ill during the spring. A further blow was to fall in July 1531. The court was at Windsor and Henry rode out one day with Anne at his side. He did not return. As was customary between the couple, following a three-day's absence Katharine wrote to him. Henry ordered her to refrain from contacting him in future either by letter or messenger and Katharine was never to see her husband again.

Orders shortly came for Katharine to remove herself to a house known as The More, in Hertfordshire. It had been one of Wolsey's houses and was therefore now in the King's hands. Although Katharine protested loudly, she was still well served and provided for and no palace of Wolsey's was likely to have been uncomfortable. Henry sent further delegations to try to persuade her to conform but it was useless – she was determined to fight for her rights and for Mary's. She now began to suggest that, rather than being motivated by genuine scruples, it was his passion for Anne Boleyn that was driving him.

Meanwhile further delays in the case were unfolding in Rome. Clement's strategy was counter-productive. An early confirmation of the validity of the marriage might well have been accepted by Henry or a firm judgement against Katharine at an early stage would have given her no option but to acquiesce. By dragging the case out, neither party was satisfied and Henry became determined to find his own way through the problem. The final rupture between Henry and Katharine came in January 1532 when, as was her custom, she sent him a New Year gift of a gold cup. The King having carefully examined the object, sent it back and ordered her desist from any further communications.

In Rome, Clement's advisers had finally come to a conclusion. Although they declined to accept Katharine's assertions as to her virginity as relevant, on the basis that this was something that could never be proven, the fact that Henry had married her of his own free will, regarded her as his wife and had children by her, rendered the marriage valid. These recommendations were not made as formal judgements.

Clement was still so reluctant to alienate Henry that, having discovered that he was living openly with Anne, rather than excommunicating him as some of Katharine's partisans wished, he merely wrote to him urging him to refrain from such improper behaviour. Again Clement could please nobody. Henry was furious, Katharine contemptuous and Chapuys scornful. A side-effect of this letter was Katharine's dispatch from The More to Ampthill in Bedfordshire, with a reduced household.

Chapter 15: Judgement

By 1532 Henry had had enough prevarication and sought to resolve the issue in England. The Convocation of clergy was forced to accept that Henry was supreme head of the Church of England with only the words *'so far as the Law of God allows'* interpolated at a late stage to fudge the issue of Papal authority.

Archbishop Warham finally woke up to the seriousness of Henry's purpose and on 24th February 1532 he protested in Parliament against any acts which might be prejudicial to Papal power or his own primacy as Archbishop. His protest was too little and too late. Henry berated him in open Parliament. Aged in his early 80s, Warham had no hope of turning back the tide and he died in the summer of 1532.

In February 1533, Parliament passed the Act in Restraint of Appeals, which prohibited any appeal to Rome against sentences passed in England. This was followed up in early April by the Convocation of clergy affirming that the Pope had no authority to grant a dispensation for a man to marry his brother's widow. Just to be on the safe side, a committee of lawyers ruled that Katharine's marriage to Arthur had been consummated.

Katharine was given one last chance to co-operate on 9th April when Henry sent a delegation of nobles, including the Dukes of Norfolk and Suffolk, to insist that she accept the jurisdiction of an English court. It was a vain hope – she reiterated that only the Pope could rule satisfactorily. The gentlemen took the opportunity to inform her that Henry had married Anne some months before and the news that Anne was pregnant would soon have reached Katharine.

Henry had seized on Warham's death to appoint Thomas Cranmer as Archbishop of Canterbury. Cranmer, who was a Fellow of Cambridge, had come to the King's attention in 1529 with his suggestion that the universities should be consulted. Following this, he had taken an active part in developing arguments to support the King's case, as well as taking part in a personal embassy to the Pope, along with two bishops. When Henry requested Cranmer's appointment as Archbishop, Clement VII was only too happy to grant at least one of the King's wishes and issued the Papal Bulls. At his consecration on 30th March 1533, Cranmer swore the customary oath to the papacy with the reservation that it should not conflict with his duties to Henry VIII as Supreme Head of the Church.

Once Archbishop, Cranmer lost no time. He convened an Archiepiscopal court at Dunstable which opened on 10 May. Katharine once again refused to appear so Cranmer proceeded to the hearings and gave judgement on 23rd May. He declared that the marriage of Henry and Katharine had been invalid from the start and that therefore when Henry had married Anne Boleyn he had been a bachelor. After seven years of wrangling Henry was free.

Anne was crowned as Queen of England on 1st June 1533. Just over a month later, Katharine's Chamberlain, Lord Mountjoy, came to her at Ampthill and informed her that she was to be known henceforth as 'Princess Dowager'. Katharine, of course, was having none of it. She reiterated her stance that she was Henry's wife, that their marriage had been legal, and that only the Pope could rule otherwise. She confirmed that whilst she would continue to obey the King in any matters which did not touch her conscience, she would not imperil her soul or that of her daughter for fear of any threats. She asked for Mountjoy's authorisation and struck out any reference to herself as Princess Dowager.

A proclamation was issued by Henry on 5th July stating that the illicit marriage between himself and the Lady Katharine, his brother's widow, had been dissolved and that he had married Lady Anne, who was now Queen of England. Any of his subjects who were so foolish as to deny either the validity of the annulment or his new marriage would be subject to penalty, as would be anybody who wrote to Katharine or referred to her or acknowledged her as Queen. Katharine was to be treated with all respect due to her royal blood and her status as Princess Dowager of Wales.

In Rome there was uproar at Henry's actions. Clement continued to vacillate but, following two days of debate by the College of Cardinals, issued a Papal Bull on 11th July 1533, declaring that Cranmer's sentence was invalid and any marriage Henry might have undertaken with Anne Boleyn was similarly void. Initially the Cardinals had suggested that Henry should be given one month to mend his ways prior to being excommunicated but Clement gave him until the end of September.

In addition, Clement accepted the advice previously given that the matter of Katharine's virginity was unprovable but stated that, as her marriage to Henry had been *public notorious and consummated* and subsisted for many years before being questioned by Henry, the King could not now claim to dispute the original dispensation. This was not a decision on the validity of the marriage itself, which he was still considering and Henry had until 1 October to make an appeal. A further Bull was issued on 8th August ordering Henry to separate from Anne and restore Katharine to her rightful position within 10 days, on pain of excommunication.

Chapter 16: Decline

During July 1533 Katharine was ordered to move again, this time to Buckden Palace in Cambridgeshire. It was while she was there that she would have heard of the birth of Anne's daughter, Elizabeth. Although Henry was, of course, disappointed at the birth of another daughter, he did immediately recognise Elizabeth as his heir and Mary lost her title of Princess. This was a blow to both mother and daughter, and was compounded when Mary was forced to join the household of her new half-sister.

Katharine, hearing of this, wrote to her daughter urging her to obey her father in all things so far as her conscience permitted and warning her not to be drawn into argument about the annulment. She sent her two Latin prayer books and urged her to find comfort in music. Emphasising her own position she signed the letter 'Katharine the Queen'.

Katharine's household was reduced further, and her servants were interrogated about their methods of addressing her. Lord Mountjoy who had served her for many years, was supposed to ensure the conformity with the rules. Distressed by pull of loyalties he tried unsuccessfully to resign his office.

In December 1533, Charles Brandon, Duke of Suffolk, Katharine's former brother-in-law, came to Buckden with the news that she was to move to the Castle at Somersham, a notoriously unhealthy place deep in the Fens. Further, she was only to be served by people who referred to her as Princess Dowager. Once again Katharine dug her heels in. She absolutely refused to move to Somersham on the basis that to do so would be tantamount to suicide, nor would she accept any servant who did not address her correctly.

Suffolk was between a rock and a hard place. He was disobeying the King if he permitted any servants to remain who referred to Katharine as Queen, but she refused to have anything to do with those who would not. Eventually her doctor, her apothecary and her confessor, who were all Spanish, and two women were left. Katharine, always with a flair for the dramatic, locked herself into her room to prevent being carried away to Somersham by force.

On 23rd March 1534, Clement finally ruled on the matter of the matrimony between Henry and Katharine, declaring it to have been lawful. Once again it was too little and too late. Charles had neither the time money nor inclination to enforce the sentence militarily: he would not even use trade sanctions to encourage Henry to conform.

Whether by coincidence or planning, on the same day that the sentence was delivered, the English Parliament passed the first Act of Succession, confirming the validity of Henry and Anne's marriage and naming Elizabeth as his successor. The use of the title Queen for Katharine was now prohibited by law. After the 1st May 1534 anyone questioning the validity of Henry and Anne's marriage was to be deemed guilty of high treason.

Having been defeated on the matter of sending Katharine to Somersham, Henry now chose to send her to Kimbolton Castle. Presumably this was not so notoriously unhealthy and Katharine cooperated. Two bishops were sent to her to inform her that if she failed to swear to the Act of Succession all the penalties of the law would be brought against her. There is no record of whether she was actually specifically asked to take the oath.

Further delegations and exhortations from Henry's Councillors including Sir Edmund Bedingfield, who was appointed as Katharine's guardian and gaoler at Kimbolton, were equally fruitless but she was not pursued with the full rigour of the law. Her supporters, Thomas More and John Fisher, were not so fortunate, both eventually being executed for upholding Papal Supremacy.

In September 1534 Clement died and was replaced by Paul III. Initially it seemed that Paul might look more favourably on Henry's case but yet again European politics intervened. The Emperor Charles won an overwhelming victory at the Battle of Cagliarli off the coast of Africa in the greatest victory over Suleiman the Magnificent's forces that Christendom had yet achieved. Whilst this may have appeared to benefit Katharine, Charles was far too busy to contemplate sending an army to England.

Katharine was miserable and alone. In spring 1535 she learned that her daughter Mary was in declining health. Having been forbidden to write directly to the King, she wrote to Chapuys asking him to plead with Henry to allow Mary to be with her to be nursed with her own hands. Katharine promised on pain of her own death that, if Mary were with her, she would not encourage her daughter to try to escape from England. Nevertheless, Henry rejected the plea although he relented so far as to permit Mary to move to a house sufficiently close for the two women to share a doctor.

Chapter 17: The End

Towards the end of 1535 it became apparent that Katharine was dying. She was unable to hold down food and suffering from violent pains in her stomach. On hearing this, her old friend Maria de Salinas talked her way into Kimbolton by pretending to have had a riding accident on her way to visit with the King's permission.

Henry permitted Chapuys to visit the dying woman and Katharine was considerably cheered by his visit, holding a number of conversations with him. Apparently the substance of her remarks related to her concerns for her daughter, her disappointment at the Pope's dilatoriness in reaching sentence and her concerns that her actions had led to heresy gaining a foothold in England. As Katharine considered herself to be a married woman she could not make a will without her husband's consent. Instead, she dictated a short list of her requests which she gave to Chapuys, this included the bequeathing of her furs and a golden collar that she had brought from Spain to Mary.

Rallying in the few days of his visit, she relapsed after his departure. Reaching the end, she may have dictated a last letter to Henry. Her biographer Giles Tremlett questions the authenticity as there is no contemporaneous, authenticated document. Nevertheless, most other biographers have accepted the versions or references to it published in the 16th century as indicating that such a letter once existed.

Katharine died early in the morning of Friday, 7th January 1536. As was customary her body was opened and disembowelled. It was recorded by the embalmer that her heart was *'quite black and hideous to look at'* with a black lump attached to it. This has been interpreted as indicating death from some form of cancer.

On hearing the news, Henry and Anne displayed a tasteless display of delight, dressing in yellow and dancing.

Orders were given for Katharine to be buried with the honour suitable for a daughter of Spain and a Dowager Princess of Wales. She lay in the chapel at Kimbolton, where masses were sung, attended by ladies of the court, including the Duchess of Suffolk, daughter of her old friend Maria de Salinas, and the Countesses of Worcester, Oxford and Surrey. On 29th January her funeral took place at Peterborough Abbey (now a Cathedral).

The chief mourner was Lady Eleanor Brandon, Henry's niece, and other mourners included Lady Bedingfield of Oxburgh Hall.

The spot is marked today with a stone paid for by public subscription in the 19th century, following an appeal to all of the Katharines/Katherines/Catherines etc of England. The banners and arms of Spain and England displayed were set up on the orders of Queen Mary of Teck in the 20th century. An annual commemoration is held at Peterborough Cathedral for a queen who was much loved by the people of England.

Part 2: Aspects of Katharine of Aragon's Life

Chapter 18: Following the Footsteps of Katharine of Aragon

In Katharine's youth, she travelled extensively in Spain, but when she left the enchanted palace of the Alhambra, she can have had little idea of what lay ahead of her. Once in England, she spent the short months of her first marriage in the Welsh Marches, in a castle that had security rather than comfort as its main function. Later though, she was to live in some of the most up to date palaces in England before she was banished from court in 1531 and relegated once again to a damp and draughty keep.

The numbers in the article below correspond to those on the map which follows.

*

Katharine was born not far from Madrid in the centre of modern day Spain in the town of Alcalá de Henares. Much of her childhood was spent travelling up and down the country as her parents sought to establish their authority and to conquer the kingdom of Granada – the last remnants of the Moorish conquest of A.D. 711.

In 1499, the royal family settled in the Alhambra, the fairy-tale palace which is now a World Heritage site – it was a scene of beauty and sophistication that even the most modern and harmonious of the Tudor palaces built in Katharine's lifetime could never match.

In the autumn of 1501, Katharine set sail for England, with the intention of landing in Southampton. Storms blew her little fleet off course and the Princess arrived in Plymouth (1) on 8th October. Then, as now, Plymouth was a naval town. Katharine showed an interest in ships and the navy throughout her time as Henry's queen, so Plymouth's superb harbour was probably a welcome sight, not just as an escape from a terrible crossing. Her first action after disembarking was to go to the nearest church to give God thanks for her safe arrival.

The Princess rested in Plymouth for some days before beginning her journey towards London. Progress was slow and it was not until 6th November that she reached the palace of the Bishop of Bath and Wells at Dogmersfield (2), near Odiham in Hampshire. It was there that she first set eyes on her future husband, Arthur, Prince of Wales. Nothing remains of Dogmersfield today, and even its exact location is not certain. Arthur and his father, Henry VII, preceded the Princess to London to ensure that all was ready for her arrival.

Katharine's journey ended in Southwark, on the south side of the Thames, almost opposite the royal palace of Westminster. She was the guest of Henry Deane, Archbishop of Canterbury, in his great palace of Lambeth (3) which is still the official residence of the Archbishop today.

On 14th November, Katharine and Arthur were married in St Paul's Cathedral (4). The day was no doubt selected because it was the Feast of St Erkenwald, the seventh century bishop whose tomb in St Paul's was a place of pilgrimage. The church that Katharine knew deteriorated in the sixteenth century, St Erkenwald's shrine was demolished in Edward VI's reign, and the steeple was badly damaged by lightening in 1561. The whole cathedral was burnt to the ground during the Great Fire of London in 1666. The current replacement, the masterpiece of architect Sir Christopher Wren, was completed in 1708 during the reign of Queen

Anne.   It was at St Paul's Cathedral that public thanksgivings or commemorations were held, and it was there that Luther's works were burnt in 1521. In 1525 Henry and Katharine went in procession to St Paul's to celebrate the capture of François I, by the Emperor Charles, at the Battle of Pavia.

Not long after they were married the decision was taken that Katharine and Arthur would travel to the marches of Wales where Arthur had been living on and off for several years. Arthur's role was to preside over the Council of Wales and the Marches as a preparation for kingship. He had a number of houses in the area but Ludlow Castle (5) was his main seat and it was there that he and Katharine went early in the New Year of 1502. The winter and spring of 1502 appear to have been wetter and colder than usual and it's not difficult to imagine that Katharine heartily wished herself in sunny Spain.

Whether she was happy in her married life we can never know. Her later assertions that she and Arthur did not consummate their marriage and the implication she gave that it was on account of his youth suggest that the young couple were hardly Romeo and Juliet. Nevertheless her husband's death must have been a blow to her, if only for the reason that she had been brought up since she was four years old to believe that was her destiny to be Queen of England. Returning home as a widow at the age of 16 might have felt like failure.

An initial request by Katharine's mother, Queen Isabella, for her daughter to return home was quickly followed up by beginning of negotiations for Katharine to remain in England to marry Arthur's younger brother, Henry, now heir to the throne. Katharine returned to London and spent the next seven years either in rooms at the court – usually Richmond or Windsor - or at Durham House (6) in the Strand.

Durham House had been built in the 1220s and was on the westernmost edge of the city of London, bordering on Westminster. It could be accessed from the river, which was convenient as the majority of travel by the court in and around the palaces was by boat. We know that Katharine used this means of transport as there is an entry in the Privy Purse expenses of her mother-in-law, Queen Elizabeth of York, for conveying the Princess in Elizabeth's own barge pulled by 16 oarsmen. The trip was from Durham House to Westminster Palace and back again on 6 November 1502. The oarsmen received 4d each, and the master 16d.

Later, Henry preferred to minimise Katharine's expenses by requiring her to live at court although she saw little of her supposed fiancé, Prince Henry. In the late 1520s and early 1530s, Durham House was lived in by Sir Thomas Boleyn and his daughter Anne. Perhaps Anne thought of Katharine's long wait for marriage to Henry as she herself paced the gardens, running down to the Thames.

The limbo in which Katharine existed following her widowhood became a paradise in 1509 when Henry VII died and the new king, Henry VIII, to whom she had been betrothed for six years immediately claimed as his wife. The couple married on 11th June 1509 at the Palace of Placentia, Greenwich. (6) This palace had originally been built by Humphrey, Duke of Gloucester in the early 1400s, and was a great favourite with both Katharine and Henry. It was here that their daughter was born in February 1516.

In the early years of Henry and Katharine's marriage, they spent a good deal of time at Richmond Palace (7), which had been comprehensively rebuilt by Henry VII following the destruction by fire of the old Palace of Sheen. It was at Richmond that Katharine and Henry's son, Henry, Duke of Cornwall, was born and lived for eight short weeks.

Little remains of Richmond now, other the red brick ruins of Henry VII's gatehouse (with his arms recently restored) and a courtyard of largely 18th and 19th century houses in Tudor style. It was at Richmond that the Tudor age finally closed when Elizabeth I, daughter of Katharine's rival, Anne Boleyn, died there in 1603. Although the Jacobean court of King James, Queen Anne and Prince Henry of Wales frequently visited, as time passed the Palace fell into disuse and much was sold off under the Commonwealth.

During the happy years of their marriage, Katharine and Henry had many interests in common, including a taste for chivalry and romance. Henry took the quasi-religious status of the Order of the Garter very seriously. He ordered the construction of an oriel window in King Edward IV's chapel on the north side of the quire in St George's Chapel Windsor (8), from which Katharine was able to watch the Garter ceremonies. The window, which has been redecorated with her arms, was the location from which Queen Victoria watched the wedding of her son Edward, Prince of Wales, to Alexandra of Denmark in 1863.

If Katharine's ghost walks at Windsor she is able to look down and see the tombstone marking the grave of Henry VIII and his third wife, Jane Seymour. Henry had originally intended that he and Katharine would be interred in a sumptuous tomb at Westminster Abbey but that was obviously no longer appropriate after Henry had his marriage to Katharine annulled. Although Henry and Katharine were not to be buried together, it was at Windsor that she last saw him in the summer of 1531. The court was in residence when Henry rode out hunting one day, accompanied by Anne Boleyn. He gave orders that Katharine was to leave before he returned.

St George's Chapel is open to the public today and more information can be found about access on the Windsor Castle website.

In 1526, Henry began to question the validity of his marriage to Katharine. After a good deal of delay by the Pope amidst an ever-changing European political scene, a court was opened, presided over by Cardinals Wolsey and Campeggio to try the case. The hearing took place at the Priory of Blackfriars (9) in London. The Priory, which was a Dominican house, was an important landmark in London and was frequently used for meetings of Parliament and the King's Council. It was a popular site for courtiers to be interred, amongst them Sir Thomas Parr in 1517 and his wife Maud Green, Lady Parr, in 1531. Lady Parr had been one of Katharine's ladies in waiting and her daughter, Katharine Parr, married Henry in 1543.

It was during the court hearing that Katherine staged the scene for which she will be forever remembered. Refusing to recognise the validity of the court, she crossed from her seat and knelt before her husband proclaiming the validity of their marriage, her faithfulness as a wife and the lack of blame that could be imputed to her for the loss of their children. Despite this dramatic plea, Henry did not relent.

Blackfriars Priory was dissolved in 1538 and on 12th March 1550 at least part of it was granted to Sir Thomas Cawarden, who was Edward VI's Master of the Revels. Further associations with the theatre continued – Blackfriars Theatre was owned by Shakespeare and his partners in The Lord Chamberlain's Men. When a dispute with the landlord arose, they picked up the building to move it from Blackfriars to Southwark, where it became known as the Globe Theatre. During Elizabeth's reign, Sir William Cecil had a property at Blackfriars and a number of his letters are dated from there.

Like many of the religious houses that once dotted London, Blackfriars is remembered today in a number of place names – most obviously the Blackfriars Bridge and Blackfriars station. The location of these marks the south east corner of the original Priory lands.

When Katharine was ordered to leave Windsor in 1531, she was sent to a house called The More (11) in Hertfordshire, which had been owned by Cardinal Wolsey in his capacity as Abbot of St Albans. Wolsey spent considerable sums of money on this, as well as on his other houses, improving the lodgings and laying out gardens. The house was sufficiently impressive for it to be the location of the signing of the Treaty of The More between England and France in August 1525 and it was compared very favourably with Hampton court.

Thus, when Katharine was sent there in 1531 it was not intended that her dignity and status should be seriously diminished. After Katharine had left in 1532, Henry frequently used the property and spent considerable sums on both buildings and gardens, creating separate King's and Queen's lodgings. It was also used by Edward VI but was not favoured by either Mary or Elizabeth. It appears that the property suffered from subsidence and by the time it was granted in 1576 to the Earl of Bedford, it was in some decay, and considered ruinous 20 years later. The Earl built himself a new house known as Moor Park which is still extant. This is the Moor Park famous for the apricots that readers of Jane Austen will remember were boasted of by Mrs Norris in *Mansfield Park*. The site of the Palace that Katharine would have known was extensively excavated in the early 1950s.

When Henry ordered that Katharine should leave The More, she was sent to Ampthill (12). Ampthill today is a busy town in Bedfordshire - the old High Street is recognisably mediaeval in origin. Ampthill Castle was originally been built by Sir John Cornwall, husband of Elizabeth of Lancaster, and thus brother-in-law to King Henry IV. It came into Henry VIII's possession in 1524.

The Castle, where Katharine was lodged, was located in what is today Ampthill Park to the north of the town. What is believed to be its location is marked by a monument called the *'Katharine Cross'*, erected in 1770s. The wording originally inscribed on the cross was said to be by Horace Walpole:

> *In days of old here* Ampthill's *towers were seen,*
> *The mournful refuge of an injured Queen;*
> *Here flowed her pure but unavailing tears,*
> *Here blinded zeal sustain'd her sinking years.*
> *Yet Freedom hence her radiant banner wav'd,*
> *And Love aveng'd a realm by priests enslav'd;*
> *From Catherine's wrongs a nation's bliss was spread,*
> *And Luther's light from Henry's lawless bed.*

Katharine's sojourn at Ampthill was not long, but whilst she was resident in the county of Bedfordshire, Archbishop Thomas Cranmer opened a court at Dunstable Priory (12) in May 1533, at which her marriage was declared invalid.

The parish Church of St Peter at Dunstable was begun in the 1130s and completed some twenty years later. Early in the next century, a house of Augustinian friars was attached to it. The friary was dissolved in 1547, but the church remained to serve the parish and is still standing.

Katharine was no longer considered by Henry to be his queen, and with the legal justification given by Cranmer for demoting her status, she could now be treated more harshly. In 1533 she was sent to Buckden (13) in Cambridgeshire. Today there is almost a direct road between Ampthill and Buckden, the A660. This probably follows the route that Katharine would have taken, travelling north-east, skirting Bedford and crossing the modern A1 to join the old Great North Road which runs directly through the town of Buckden. It is a pleasant and easy drive today, more interesting than the A1.

Buckden Palace was in the possession of the Bishops of Lincoln and was of sufficient stature to have been used from time to time by Henry's grandmother, Lady Margaret Beaufort. Sufficient elements of the late 15th century palace remain to give a strong impression of the building in which Katharine passed many unhappy months. It is a pleasant enough place in spring or summer but in winter, with the wind whistling over the flat fields of Cambridgeshire, it must have been bitterly cold. It was, however, on the main road, and not isolated in the fens, which was the situation of Somersham castle, to which Katharine was ordered to move in 1534. She adamantly refused to go somewhere so unhealthy, locking herself in her room at Buckden, probably in the tower that can still be seen. Henry's commission did not dare to take her by force.

Having refused to move to Somersham, the decision was taken that Katharine must go to Kimbolton Castle (14). Kimbolton is situated about nine miles back towards Bedford on the A660. It is another charming English town with a mixture of 18th and 19th century façades on properties that are probably several hundred years older. Kimbolton Castle itself is now a vast 18th century mansion, housing a school. Inside there are traces of the buildings as they would have been in Katharine's time, but they are not always accessible to the public.

Katharine died at Kimbolton on 7th January 1536. On the 27th of the month her body left Kimbolton to make its final journey, stopping overnight at Sawtry before arriving at Peterborough Abbey (15), as it then was, on 29th January, and being interred the same day.

Visitors to Peterborough Cathedral today will see a black marble monument which was erected in the 19th century, paid for by subscriptions from ladies shared Katharine's Christian name in its many varieties of spelling. The words '*Katharine the Queen*' are affixed to the grill above the monument in recognition of Katharine's much loved memory.

The list below corresponds to the map which follows of places Katharine would have known.

Key to Map

1. Plymouth, Devon
2. Dogmersfield, Hampshire
3. Lambeth Palace, Southwark, London
4. St Paul's Cathedral, London
5. Ludlow Castle, Shropshire
6. Durham House, London
7. Greenwich, London
8. Richmond, London
9. Blackfriar's London
10. St George's Chapel, Windsor
11. The More, Hertfordshire
12. Dunstable Priory, Bedfordshire,
13. Buckden Palace, Cambridgeshire
14. Kimbolton Castle, Cambridgeshire
15. Peterborough Abbey, Camridgeshire

Map

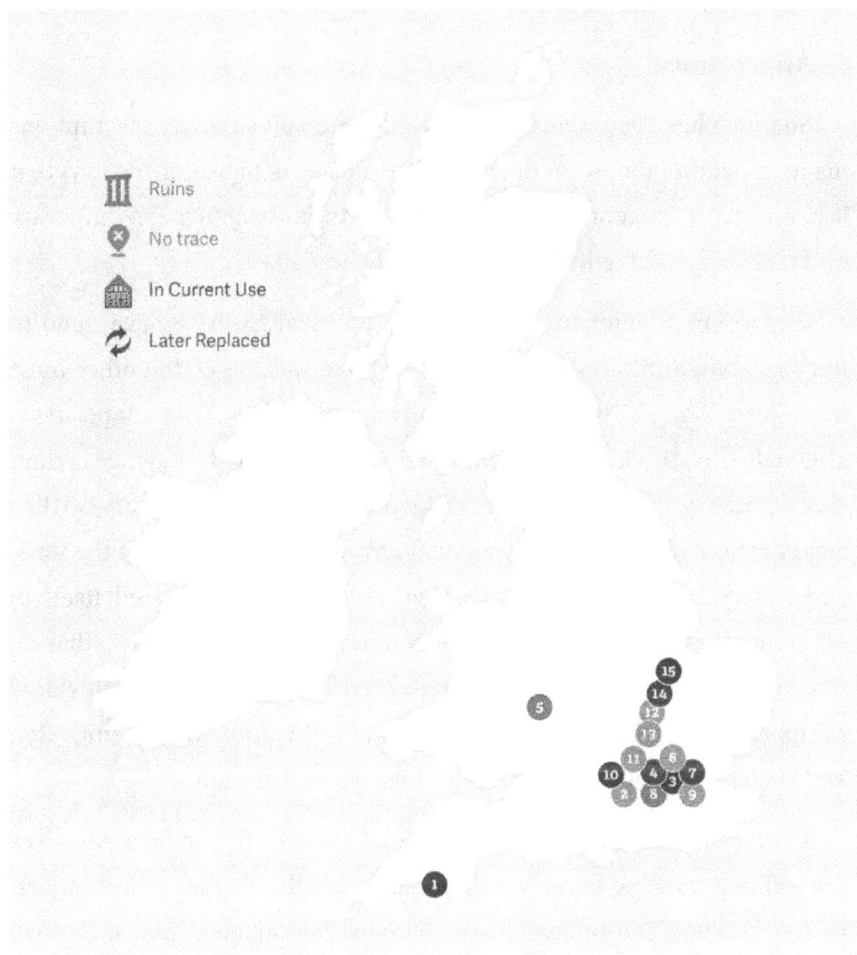

Ruins

No trace

In Current Use

Later Replaced

Chapter 19: Appearance and Character

Appearance

So much has been written about Katharine and so many assumptions made in fiction (and, sometimes, in what purports to be non-fiction) that it is very hard to ignore everything and try to find enough contemporary evidence to give some insight into what she was like.

In particular, comparisons with her successor, Anne Boleyn, tend to put the women into opposing camps – if one was '*good*' the other must have been '*bad*'. They are frequently presented as polar opposites – although we think a case can be made for them having certain characteristics in common – a willingness to challenge Henry VIII, a stubbornness that would have seen off any lesser woman in half the time, and a very high level of intelligence, although it manifested itself in different ways. We have tried here to identify descriptions of Katharine that are contemporaneous, and to indicate what the bias of an individual commentator might have been – although that is fraught with difficulty, and presented as our tentative view, not a definitive truth.

Katharine's first appearance to English eyes was when she was present at a meeting between her parents, and the English ambassadors, in March 1489. The ambassadors – Richard Nanfan and Thomas Savage, were being presented to Ferdinand and Isabella at Medina del Campo, where Katharine had been born. Their account of the visit dwells on the unbelievable splendour of Queen Isabella's clothes and magnificent jewellery. Katharine herself, with her older sister, Maria, was in a small room, surrounded by their fourteen youthful maids-of-honour. Katharine, only three, was too young to dance, but Maria showed off the training that both were receiving in this important courtly skill. The following day, the children were present at a bull-fight, Isabella holding her youngest in her arms to watch the scene.

Katharine's next recorded appearance on the public stage came some eight years later when, dressed in cloth-of-gold, she waited with her siblings to greet the Archduchess Marguerite of Austria, who had come from Burgundy, in exchange for Katharine's own sister, Juana. Marguerite was to marry Juan, the heir to the Spanish thrones.

In the strict hierarchy so important to the Spanish court, Katharine was positioned lower on the staircase than her sisters, but above her father's illegitimate daughter (who Ferdinand was offering to James IV of Scotland as a potential bride). Katharine's biographer, Giles Tremlett, suggests that the paintings by Juan de Flandres of the Spanish Infantas may date from this period.

The death of Juan within a year of marrying the exotic French-educated archduchess, blamed on over-exertion in the marital bed, must have shocked Katharine profoundly, and perhaps influenced her marriage to Arthur. Further misery was heaped on the family when Marguerite had a miscarriage.

In 1501, it was Katharine's turn to travel to a foreign land, to an unknown husband. On arriving in London, she processed riding a richly-harnessed mule, to St Paul's Cathedral for her wedding. Her dress and appearance are not described in detail, other than to note that she wore a hat like a cardinal's (that is, broad-brimmed, with a low crown), and that beneath this, her hair flowed over her shoulders. Sir Thomas More (who was present) was later to say that few women could compare for looks with Katharine in her youth, but frustratingly, there is no specific description.

It has long been affirmed that, contrary to the usual dark complexion of Spaniards, Katharine was fair – hardly surprising that she might not conform to the looks of many Spaniards when, like most royalty, her heritage was rather more multi-national.

As evidence for this, there is only one certain portrait – that of Lucas Horenbout. This dates to the mid-1520s. The Juan de Flandres painting is not definitively of Katharine, and the picture long accepted as Katharine in youth by Michel Sittow, is now named as probably her sister-in-law, Mary, daughter of Henry VII, later Queen of France.

All of the other pictures that are named as representing Katharine show her with the gable hood which covered the hair.

The Queen's hair seems to have been the aspect of her appearance that was most admired. Hall's Chronicle, recalling the coronation of the royal couple, describes it as *'of a very great length...beautiful and goodly to behold.'*

Just after her marriage to Henry in 1509, Katharine was described, perhaps somewhat partially, by her Confessor, Fray Diego:

'Her highness is very healthy and the most beautiful creature in the world, with the greatest gaiety and contentment that ever was.'

In 1512, Henry is recorded as kissing and caressing her in public, and, according to a Spanish source, he would invite guests to admire his beautiful wife.

Perhaps a rather less partial view was taken by a Venetian visitor to the court in 1515. She was by then 30 years old and is described, rather unchivalrously, and not, presumably, by anyone expecting to have his correspondence read, other than by the recipient, as

'ugly and deformed.'

This seems a harsh judgement, as the next description, from 1519, by another Venetian, Sebastian Giustinian, records that Katharine was:

'35 years old, and not handsome, though she ha[s] a very beautiful complexion. She [is] religious, and as virtuous as words could express.'

We have a brief glimpse of Katharine's clothes, if not her looks, in 1520, when her nephew, the Emperor Charles V, paid a state visit to England, accompanied by Germaine de Foix, Katharine's step-mother, the widowed Queen of Aragon (reputed, shockingly, to be the mistress of Charles, her step-grandson.)

'The Queen's petticoat was of silver lama [lamé?], and the gown of cloth of gold lined with violet velvet, with raised pile, on which the roses of England were wrought in gold. She wore a necklace of very large pearls, from which hung a very valuable diamond cross. Her head gear was of black velvet striped with gold lama, and powdered with jewels and pearls.'

Other fabulous gowns were in Katharine's wardrobe – gold tissue, black tilsent (a type of shot silk) decorated with katherine-wheels and cloth of silver. She was certainly a match for Henry in a taste for magnificence and display – hardly the dowdy frump of legend!

Despite this impressive appearance, a year later, following the Field of the Cloth of Gold, King François informed the Venetian embassy that the King of England was *'young and handsome'* but that his wife was *'old and deformed'*. Of course, François was no more inclined to like a Spaniard, than Katharine was to appreciate a French king.

From François' cruel words, we can perhaps infer that the pretty girl that Katharine once was had lost her looks in the battle to survive seven pregnancies, and the grief of losing all her children but one.

The companion portraits of Henry and Katharine at Lambeth Palace date from around this time.

The last description of Katharine's appearance dates from 1531, after she had been sent to The More, but was still treated as Queen and allowed to receive foreign visitors. Yet a third Venetian wrote, rather more chivalrously:

'Her Majesty is not of tall stature, rather small. If not handsome, she is not ugly: she is somewhat stout and has always a smile on her face.'

The latter comment is surprising, as, by that time, Katharine had little to smile about!

Character

As to character, the overwhelming impression that Katharine leaves is that she was utterly single-minded. What she set her mind on, she never deviated from pursuing.

What can be ascertained from contemporary sources is that she never forgot a friend or an enemy – a maid-of-honour who had disobeyed her during the years as Arthur's widow, by marrying without consent, was never forgiven. On being asked for the equivalent of a reference for Francesca, Katharine refused. Similarly, her former tutor and confessor, Alessandro Grinaldi, incurred her wrath to the extent that, fifteen years after he left her service, she refused to receive him.

On the positive side, Katharine was loyal to those who served her – much of her correspondence relates to recommending her friends and servants. This was a necessary part of her role as Queen, but even her will shows real concern for the welfare of her remaining attendants – requesting extra wages for them.

The years of her widowhood show Katharine as emotional, and prone to despair – perhaps not unusual for a girl in her teens – it is easy to forget that adolescents of the sixteenth century were just as affected by hormonal changes as modern youth. She dealt with her troubles by prayer, excessive fasting, and an over-involved emotional relationship with her confessor, Fray Diego, whom she adamantly refused to dismiss, despite the rumours circulating about his licentious private life.

Once Katharine was Queen, her emotions seem to have been on a more even keel – perhaps the natural effects of maturity. Although she is recorded as lamenting sorely at the death of her son, there is no sign of the immoderate grief her sister displayed on the loss of her husband (transporting his coffined body with her for over ten years!).

Nevertheless, a flair for the dramatic certainly never left her – the dispatch of James IV's bloodstained tunic, the speech at Blackfriars, the defiance in the face of demands that she move to the damp and unhealthy castle at Somersham that led her to lock herself in her room and say she would have to be dragged out, and even the request to Henry to let her nurse their sick daughter when she told him that if Mary tried to escape England he could do justice on her as the 'most evil woman ever born.'

In the early days of their marriage, Henry relied on Katharine's advice – she was five and a half years older than him, and had more experience of diplomacy, through having acted as her father's accredited ambassador. It is apparent that during her years as Queen, foreign emissaries were aware of her influence – there are many records of instructions to wait upon the Queen, and notes about her influence on Henry. In 1513, she was quite as eager for war with France as Henry – talking to the Venetians about building or chartering suitable ships for the nascent English navy, which could be taken into battle. She is described as 'very warm in favour of this expedition.'

Later in that year, when Henry was campaigning in France and James IV of Scotland invaded England, she was willing – even eager – to march with her troops herself. When James was defeated, she would have liked to send his body to France as a trophy, but *'our Englishmen's hearts would not suffer it.'* From this we can infer that she was as imbued with the militarism of the age as anyone, and certainly not averse to war. But that was her role as queen – as a woman, she sympathised with her now-widowed sister-in-law, Margaret, Queen of Scots, and on 18th October, some five weeks after the battle, sent messages of condolence, which Margaret seems to have believed were sent in a genuine spirit of kindness.

When the meeting at the Field of Cloth of Gold was planned, she made her dislike of the plan to meet the French King in a spirit of amity known. Charles V's envoy told his master that the meeting was *'against the will of the Queen and all of the nobles'*. When the French King's mother questioned the English ambassador as to Katharine's lack of enthusiasm for a French alliance, the envoy had to fall back on her eagerness to do the King's pleasure in all things, rather than any real urge to make peace with the old enemy. Perhaps it is not surprising that King François denigrated her personal charms!

As to Katharine's intellectual capabilities, she was highly praised by Erasmus on several occasions. Erasmus was forever on the lookout for patrons, and frequently heaped praise on people in one letter, in the hope of extracting some funds, whilst delivering a snide comment in another to a friend, but, absent any evidence of derogatory comments, it is worth considering his statement:

'The Queen is well instructed – not merely in comparison with her own sex and is no less to be respected for her piety than her erudition.'

Erasmus was not the only humanist with whom Katharine had contact – Sir Thomas More, John Colet and Bishop Fisher were supported by her, as was Juan Luis Vives, the Spanish scholar whom she commissioned to draw up a plan of education for her daughter, Mary.

Katharine's skill in argument and ready intellect were well known to even her enemies. Apparently, Anne Boleyn told Henry never to argue with Katharine, as she would surely get the better of him – poor Henry, trapped between them!

Katharine took seriously her Christian duty of charity towards the poor – this also meshed with mediaeval ideas of '*good-lordship*' – a master or mistress' duty to be liberal with gifts and money. Henry VIII and their daughter, Mary, shared this trait – noticeably missing in Henry VII and Elizabeth I who were distinctly parsimonious.

The Queen's accounts show that she spent some five per cent of her income on charitable works, with five times that amount expended on gifts for her affinity. She also gave generous tips to people who brought her small gifts of cakes or flowers as she travelled between palaces.

Books of Hours were given as presents by both Katharine's mother-in-law, Elizabeth of York, and, it seems, Katharine herself. According to her biographer, Tremlett, in one she inscribed the following message:

'*I think the prayers of a friend the most acceptable and because I take you for one of mine...I pray you remember me in yours.*'

Two of the most enduring descriptions of Katharine come from her husband, and his minister, Thomas Cromwell - both determined to break her spirit and force her to accept the annulment, although neither succeeded and one can't help feeling that no matter how frustrating her stonewall tactics were, they had a deep respect for her.

According to Henry,

'*for were the Lady Katharine, who is a proud and intractable woman, to take into her head to favour her daughter, she might well take the field, raise assemblies of men, and carry on war against him as openly and fiercely as queen [Isabella], her mother, did in Spain.*'

Whilst the Imperial Ambassador reported that Cromwell had observed that:

'God and nature had done great injury to the said queen in not making her a man, for she might have surpassed in glory and fame all the princes whose heroic deeds are recorded in history.'

Katharine was not the patient saint of many stories, she was certainly capable of diplomatic lies and dissimulation, but she was also a woman of great faith and steadfastness, so we should perhaps leave her the last word, as she knelt before the husband of twenty years who sought to cast her off:

'Sir I beseech you for all the love that hath been between us and for the love of God, let me have justice....I have been to you a true, humble and obedient wife..'

Chapter 20: Katharine of Aragon in Fact and Fiction

Katharine probably appears more frequently in histories, both serious and lightheaded, than any other queen in history save, perhaps, her rival, Anne Boleyn.

So far as biography is concerned, unusually for a woman, so far in the 20th and 21st centuries, she has attracted only male biographers.

Garrett Mattingley's 1942 *Catherine of Aragon* has been the standard work for over sixty years. It can still be found in libraries and bought second hand, but is no longer in print.

In the last five years, two new biographies have appeared – Giles Tremlett's *Catherine of Aragon: Henry's Spanish Queen* and Patrick

Williams' *Katharine of Aragon: The Tragic Story of Henry VIII's first unfortunate wife.* Both are reviewed in Chapter 21, so suffice to say that they look at Katharine from a much more international viewpoint, as at the heart of the political alliance with Spain.

As an important woman in the European stage in the sixteenth century, Katharine is prominent in the various contemporary and near-contemporary chronicles and records of the time. There is a raft of diplomatic correspondence surrounding arrangements for her marriage to Arthur and then negotiations for marriage to Henry. A number of her own letter are also preserved.

So far as books or pamphlets are concerned, she first appears in *The Receyte of the Lady Kateryne,* probably written in the early sixteenth century, describing her reception in London in 1501.

She appears in the following works, published after her death, between about the end of Henry's reign (Hall) and the 1580s: George Cavendish's *Life of Wolsey,* Hall's *Chronicle,* Polydore Vergil's *Anglica Historiae,* Nicholas Harpsfield's *'The Treatise touching the pretended divorce between King Henry the Eight and Queen Katherine'* , Nicholas Sanders' *'De Origine ac Progressu Schismatis Anglicani'* , Holinshed's Chronicle, and John Foxe's *Book of Martyrs.*

In them, Katharine own character is treated overwhelmingly favourably, even by the supporters of the Reformation and the Protestants of the next generation who maintain that her marriage to Arthur was consummated. For the Catholic writers she is little short of a saint. This picture of a courageous woman, battling against the overwhelming power of her husband and his ministers, reaches its culmination in Shakespeare and his fellow author, John Fletcher's, portrayal in Henry VIII.

Each age requires its heroes and heroines to reflect its own world view and preoccupations, thus in the sixteenth century, Katharine was a martyr for her faith, by the nineteenth century she is a model of domestic faith and virtue in the evergreen *Lives of the Queens of England* and by the mid twentieth century she is a side note in the serious business of male politics.

In the twenty-first century, opinion is divided. In a non-religious age some historians, notably Dr David Starkey, have no problem believing that Katharine repeatedly lied on oath, and in the confessional about the consummation of her first marriage. Katharine's obfuscation with her father over her first miscarriage, and a willingness to indulge in the usual diplomatic practices of half-truths and possibly misleading statements, are used to support this interpretation.

Modern pragmatists in a non-religious age believe she should have accepted the annulment and retired rich and comfortable – rather as Anne of Cleves did. A more feminist agenda is torn between admiration for her courage, and disappointment that she stood for so long in the way of Anne Boleyn, whose temperament seems more in tune with our own times.

There are a number of joint biographies. *The Six Wives of Henry VIII* (Alison Weir) and *The Six Wives of Henry VIII* (Antonia Fraser (the latter in particular) are overwhelmingly favourable. Starkey in *Six Wives: The Queens of Henry VIII* is generally less so, highlighting less favourable interpretations of many of Katharine's actions (Katharine crying when Henry told her he was seeking a divorce was '*no doubted intended*' to unman him). Still, it is good to hear a different perspective.

Amy Licence in *The Six Wives and Many Mistresses of Henry VIII* gives some fascinating background detail on childbirth customs and

Katharine's general gynaecological health. With a wider focus on Henry's love-life, Katharine is not the focus.

England's Queens by Elizabeth Norton, gives a good summary of the facts of Katharine's life.

Professor David Loades, in his *Tudor Queens of England* sums up the argument that Katharine should have accepted the annulment. Whilst he acknowledges that Katharine believed herself to be acting on principle, he does identify that her motives had the very human attribute of resentment at the thought of being supplanted by Anne Boleyn.

In fiction, the classic is Norah Lofts' *The King's Pleasure*, a beautifully written work which exposes the emotional pain of the annulment. Alison Weir's *Katherine of Aragon: The True Queen* (5 May 2016) has a similar perspective. Jean Plaidy's old three decker I find drags a little. Philippa Gregory's *The Constant Princess* is popular, but I wanted to throw it across the room as ahistorical.

Hilary Mantel treads an interesting line in *Wolf Hall*. It is clear that Cromwell can admire Katharine's courage, but ultimately, he thinks her a fool for holding on to a marriage that can never be revived, rather than accepting the annulment with good grace – she is eager for martyrdom and, he believes, willing to take her daughter with her, of which he disapproves.

All in all, there is a wealth of material, to suit every taste.

Chapter 21: Two Book Reviews

The magisterial biography by Mattingley written in the 1940s has not been challenged until recently, but two new biographies, by Giles

Tremlett and Patrick Williams, have given a whole new insight into Katharine, and the politics and diplomacy that surrounded her.

Title: Catherine of Aragon, Henry's Spanish Queen

Author: Giles Tremlett

Publisher: Faber & Faber

In a nutshell The use of Spanish material greatly enhances this root and branch re-evaluation of Katharine's life.

Giles Tremlett's biography of Katharine is the first major revision of her life since the 1942 work of Garrett Mattingley, which has been the authority on the Queen for sixty years, although she has, of course, been an integral part of the various joint biographies of Henry VIII's wives.

Tremlett is not a dedicated Tudor historian, rather he is a specialist on Spanish history, and this gives his work a new, and more international feel, than the joint biographies where she is seen in an English context.

The substance of Tremlett's work is Katharine's place in the wider Spanish foreign policy of surrounding France with its own allies. Initially, this was the vision of her parents, Ferdinand and and Isabella, but Tremlett demonstrates how the policy continued under Katharine's nephew, the Emperor Charles V, who valued the connection with England highly until a change in the balance of European power, and the increasing threat of Ottoman incursion into his eastern territories changed his priorities.

Charles' action in breaking off his betrothal to Katharine's daughter, Mary, is seen as pivotal in Henry's decision to seek an annulment of his marriage. The alliance had not delivered what the English king needed –

real support in his ambitions (however unrealistic) to gain the throne of France, or, at worst, the prospect of a grandson being Holy Roman Emperor. Coupled with Katharine's failure (as Henry saw it) to give him a son, her days were numbered.

Tremlett approaches the question of the consummation of Katharine's first marriage armed with previously little reported information from the Spanish archives, which, whilst it cannot be conclusive as to the secrets of the marriage bed, are still an interesting addition to the debate.

Katharine is often portrayed as a Patient Griselda figure, but Tremlett rounds out this picture by considering her weaknesses as well as her strengths – although such judgements, are, of course, subjective. He illustrates her passionate nature - using the term in its sense of deep emotional commitment, and a willingness, even an eagerness, to embrace suffering. Whilst in comparison with her sister, Juana who whether or not she was 'mad' was certainly extravagantly emotional, Katharine is calm and controlled, but her unyieldingness and certainty of purpose come across strongly. Tremlett illustrates this with information about the physical strain she put herself under during the years of widowhood – excessive prayer and fasting, which undermined her health, and became so extreme that the Pope exhorted her betrothed husband, Henry, to intervene.

This is an absorbing biography, with an interesting take on Katharine's psychology – well worth reading.

Title: Katharine of Aragon: The tragic story of Henry VIII's first, unfortunate wife

Author: Patrick Williams

Publisher: Amberley Publishing

In a nutshell This is a major contribution to an understanding of the power politics of the first third of the sixteenth century, rather than Katharine's life.

Professor Patrick Williams is Emeritus Professor of Spanish History at Portsmouth University, and his deep knowledge of the politics of sixteenth-century Spain shine through every page of this biography.

Williams has identified every action on the European stage as the kings and emperors of the Katharine's life-time sought to dominate the continent. The struggle for control of Italy, in a conflict which lasted from 1494 to 1559, was the backdrop to the Queen's life. Every twist in diplomacy, every broken treaty and each scene of senseless slaughter as France, Spain and the Papacy slugged it out in the peninsula, determined the course of Katharine's life and are meticulously recorded and analysed.

One of the things I like about the book is Williams' careful recording of the dates of events. Often, in history books there is quite a lot of '*and then...that month...that autumn*' leaving the reader confused about chronology, but Williams helpfully gives dates throughout.

The other excellent aspect of the book is the detailed exposition of the theological arguments relating to the annulment of Henry and Katharine's marriage, and the subtle meanings of the various Papal Bulls and judicial pronouncements. I did not know, for example, that the Papal court refused to pronounce on Katharine's oft-repeated statement that she and Arthur had not consummated their marriage. It was deemed by the Rota (Papal Court) to be an irrelevant point – it would be fascinating to know how Katharine felt about that.

On the downside, Williams strays too far from Katharine herself. Often, I felt the book should have been published as a biography of her nephew, Charles V, but I don't suppose it would have been attractive to publishers.

This is a super book for those wanting to read a clear and scholarly account of the politics of the time – but not so suitable for those looking for a picture of Katharine herself.

Bibliography

Brewer, John Sherren, and James Gairdner, *Letters and Papers, Foreign and Domestic, of the Reign of Henry VIII: Preserved in the Public Record Office, the British Museum, and Elsewhere in England* (United Kingdom: British History Online, 2014)

'Calendar of State Papers: Venice' <http://www.british-history.ac.uk/cal-state-papers/venice/vol2/vii-lxi> [accessed 7 October 2015]

Ellis, Henry, *Original Letters, Illustrative of English History: Including Numerous Royal Letters: From Autographs in the British Museum, the State Paper Office, and One or Two Other Collections.*, 1st edn (New York: Printed for Harding, Triphook, & Lepard, 1824)

Fraser, Antonia, *The Six Wives of Henry VIII*, 11th edn (London: Weidenfeld & Nicolson, 1993)

Hall, Edward, *Hall's Chronicle.* (S.l.: Ams Press, 1909)

Inside the Tudor Court: Henry VIII and His Six Wives through the Writings of the Spanish Ambassador Eustace Chapuys (Amberley Publishing, 2014)

Jerdan, William, *Rutland Papers. Original Documents Illustrative of the Courts and Times of Henry VII. and Henry VIII. Selected from the Private Archives of His Grace the Duke of Rutland* (Leopold Classic Library, 2015)

de Lisle, Leanda, *Tudor: The Family Story* (United Kingdom: Chatto & Windus, 2013)

Loades, David M., *The Tudor Queens of England* (London: Continuum International Publishing Group, 2009)

Mackay, Lauren, *Inside the Tudor Court: Henry VIII and His Six Wives through the Writings of the Spanish Ambassador Eustace Chapuys* (Amberley Publishing, 2014)

'Polydore Vergil: Chronicle'
<http://www.philological.bham.ac.uk/polverg/27eng.html> [accessed 2 May 2016]

Starkey, David, *Six Wives: The Queens of Henry VIII* (London: Chatto & Windus, 2002)

Tremlett, Giles, *Catherine of Aragon: Henry's Spanish Queen* (United Kingdom: Faber & Faber, 2011)

Weir, Alison, *The Six Wives of Henry VIII* (London: Random House UK Distribution, 1991)

Williams, Patrick, *Katharine of Aragon* (United Kingdom: Amberley Publishing, 2014)

http://Spain:March 1535, 16-31', in Calendar of State Papers, Spain, Volume 5 Part 1, 1534-1535, ed. Pascual de Gayangos (London, 1886), pp. 423-435. British History Online http://www.british-history.ac.uk/cal-state-papers/spain/vol5/no1/pp423-435 [accessed 4 May 2016]> [accessed 4 May 2016]

http://Spain:July 1533, 1-15', in Calendar of State Papers, Spain, Volume 4 Part 2, 1531-1533, ed. Pascual de Gayangos (London, 1882), pp. 727-741. British History Online http://www.british-history.ac.uk/cal-state-papers/spain/vol4/no2/pp727-741 [accessed 4 May 2016]> [accessed 4 May 2016]